The NFT Handbook

The NFT Handbook

How to Create, Sell and Buy
Non-Fungible Tokens

Matt Fortnow
QuHarrison Terry

WILEY

In memory of George Cowdrey, Joe Shary, John Henderson, and Robert Washington

About the Authors

As someone who has founded, built, managed, and sold a successful Internet company, **Matt Fortnow** has been in the tech startup trenches. In 1996, he cofounded Commissioner.com, the Internet's first fantasy sports service. Matt grew the company, which created fantasy sports games for the NFL, Major League Baseball, CBS SportsLine, and several others, as well as international games for soccer and cricket. In 1999, he and his partners sold the company to CBS SportsLine (currently CBS Sports), which still runs their products today.

Previously, as an entertainment lawyer, Matt co-authored the 7th Edition of *This Business of Music*, the bible of the music industry. He's represented a variety of musical artists, songwriters, producers, and record companies; appeared as a regularly featured copyright expert on television; and lectured internationally. An honors graduate of Carnegie Mellon University and a Cum Laude graduate of the Benjamin N. Cardozo School of Law, where he edited and wrote for the *Cardozo Law Review*, Matt has also written several articles on music industry issues.

Since the sale of Commissioner.com, Matt has been consulting entrepreneurs and has been involved in various startups as an investor or advisor. Six years ago, he dove into the world of blockchain, doing business development for GameCredits (GAME). In 2018, he arranged a deal between GameCredits and FanDuel, the largest fantasy sports company, for contests throughout the FIFA World Cup. Matt is cofounder of Blockchain Guys, a premier blockchain and cryptocurrency consultancy. He has become increasingly enamored by digital art and non-fungible tokens since the original CryptoKitties, and he has created the official NFTs for iconic brands such as The Three Stooges. Matt recently discussed the future of NFTs on Marketing for the Now with Gary Vaynerchuk.

QuHarrison Terry is a growth marketer at Mark Cuban Companies, a Dallas, Texas, venture capital firm, where he advises and assists portfolio companies with their marketing strategies and objectives. Previously, he led marketing at Redox, focusing on lead acquisition, new user experience, events, and content marketing. In 2015, he cofounded 23VIVI, the world's first digital art marketplace powered by the blockchain. In 2021, he sold an NFT of the Worldstar Hip-Hop Chain for 121 ETH on OpenSea.

QuHarrison has been featured on CNN, Huffington Post, Xconomy, Cointelegraph, MobiHealth News, MedCity News, and many others. As a speaker and moderator, QuHarrison has presented at CES, SXSW, TEDx, Marquette University, and the Open Data Science Conference. QuHarrison is a four-time recipient of LinkedIn's Top Voices in Technology award.

About the Technical Editor

David Hoelzer is the chief of operations for Enclave Forensics, Inc., in North America and a managing partner with Occulumen in the United Kingdom. In these roles, he oversees the day-to-day operations of Enclave's managed security monitoring functions for both network monitoring and threat hunting. David is also the principal lead for the development groups at Enclave and Occulumen, overseeing the development of a variety of custom blockchain-related technologies and covert communication technologies. He also leads Enclave's internal machine learning/AI research group. Outside of these primary roles, David serves as the dean of faculty for the SANS Technology Institute, and he has been a fellow with the SANS Institute since 2001.

Acknowledgments

With much gratitude to Danny from WorldStar Hip-Hop, Liza Wiemer, Ryan Cowdrey, Wallon Walusayi, Wendy Souter, Joe Marcus, Nigel Wyatt, Patrick Shea, Kathleen Mahoney, Coinbase, MetaMask, C3 Entertainment, Inc., Coin-MarketCap, Mike Winkelmann, Elaine O'Hanrahan, Dapper Labs, shl0ms, Scrazyone1, and WhatsGoodApps.

Thank you to anyone who has ever conversed with us about NFTs, collected NFTs alongside us, or consulted with us about their NFTs. All of those interactions helped make this book a reality.

—Matt Fortnow and QuHarrison Terry

Contents at a Glance

Contents

Foreword

Great artists focus on one thing: their creations. Musicians spend months searching for perfect harmony or lyrics, architects belabor the most minute details on their building plans, and painters search for the ideal place for their last stroke.

But once they finish their masterpieces, successful artists must also figure out how to monetize them while likewise protecting their provenance and future value.

That's where the intermediary comes in. Content creators of all kinds, including musicians, podcasters, painters, writers, performers, directors, and composers, are typically forced to use an intermediary to share their creations with the world. Whether it's the art gallery, the music label, or the concert promoter, these functionaries all promise artists the ability to monetize their work in exchange for a healthy cut of the profits—and sometimes even ownership of the artist's work.

Although not all intermediaries are bad; some have made headlines in recent years for the underhanded deals they've struck with their clients. Taylor Swift has spoken out about the unfair contract she signed as a teenager and how her music was sold multiple times without her knowledge or consent. Musicians like Prince and Michael Jackson were known for feuding with their record labels, too.

In recent years, technology platforms like Spotify have offered some hope of disintermediation. However, as the platforms evolved, artists have learned that their economics have been reduced—not enhanced. So, it's no wonder that the creative community has long sought a way to regain control—and ownership—of their valuable creative assets.

Enter the NFT, a tool that allows creators to bypass the intermediary altogether. Understanding how to harness NFT technology can put creators back in the driver's seat. At first glance, NFTs are shrouded in cryptocurrency jargon, scaring off anyone without a computer science degree, but they're relatively simple. They're a way for artists to embed a snippet of code into their works so that they can share them without fear of piracy and with the security that they will be paid directly by their supporters and fans in perpetuity. This gives them back control of their intellectual property with enhanced transparency while tracking and distributing payments to the creator for royalties and sales.

One of the most valuable parts of NFTs is the way that they allow a community to form and participate in supporting something in which they believe. In 2000, I went to my first concert in New York City to see one of my favorite bands, U2. Had they been selling NFTs that night, I might just be HODLing it for life.

Imagine having been one of the first 100 fans of U2 or having gone to a basement show and bought an NFT of a song from the next David Bowie before they blew up. The early supporters are rewarded, the artists are paid, and the community grows stronger.

It's clear now that NFTs are not only here to stay but that they stand to radically transform the creative and content industries. As a result, investing in this market is no longer a fringe idea but rather a core strategy for anybody who wants to participate in the creative economy in a meaningful way.

As an attorney who has devoted my professional career to understanding how to securitize and monetize assets in a compliant way, NFTs represent a tremendous opportunity for those who understand them.

The best time to get on the NFT bandwagon was in 2020, but the second-best time is right now. That's why I'm so excited that QuHarrison Terry and Matt Fortnow have decided to build this straightforward educational tool, opening up the possibilities of NFTs to the millions of people who make their living in creative fields. *The NFT Handbook* affords those creatives a real path to controlling their own destiny. This book is likely to become a bible for a brewing revolution.

It takes a visionary to see the future and to understand how to make it a reality. QuHarrison Terry is that visionary. He's also a businessman who began selling digital art online in 2014 and has seen firsthand how transformative this knowledge can be. Matt Fortnow has been at the forefront of the Internet revolution since his early days as an entrepreneur who built his first Internet company back in 1996, and he understands the bleeding edge of technology. Their combined experience and conviction about the future of NFTs speaks for itself. There are no two individuals more qualified to write this book.

As the CEO and cofounder of Republic, a company that also aims to demystify some of the financial world and to give people the power to invest in the future, we've gotten used to the criticism that comes with innovation. When we first started to apply traditional investment principles to crypto, some onlookers thought that we were out of our minds. Time and again, we have seen that what seems crazy today will seem normal tomorrow. (And we all wish we invested when things seemed crazy and out of favor.) The same can certainly be said for NFTs.

I cannot wait for the future that this book and this technology will bring us to. It's not if, but when.

Kendrick Nguyen
CEO and Cofounder of Republic

1

Introduction to NFTs

By many accounts, Google was late to the search engine game. Founded in 1998, it was the 24th search engine to come onto the scene. What's Google 24th at now?

Larry Page and Sergey Brin, the cofounders of Google, focused on differentiating their search engine and creating a compelling product from the outset. Monetizing the search engine was an afterthought. Search engines are all about connecting people from a query to a destination. It's a game of understanding the user's intent. What do they want to find? Ideally, the engine gets it right on the first search result; otherwise, you're forcing the user to do the hard work of finding what they're looking for.

Google's revolutionary idea was *PageRank*, a ranking system that prioritized web pages by social proof. The more that other domains link to a web page, the higher it ranked on Google's search results because there was social proof from other users that it was a helpful resource. Google's indexing method was in stark contrast to other search engines, which ranked pages by analyzing the page's content for keyword density.

Backed by this superior theory of ranking the web's content, Google showed promise of having a better utility than any other search engine of the time. It also attracted the attention of computing pioneers. Before Google was even incorporated, it received its first investment of $100,000 from Andy Bechtolsheim, cofounder of Sun Microsystems—a legend in the world of computing. Google rounded out this investment in 1998 with money from three other angel investors, including Amazon founder Jeff Bezos, Stanford University computer science professor David Cheriton, and entrepreneur Ram Shriram.

Page and Brin were just a couple of smart kids from Stanford trying to solve a problem on the Internet. Their laser focus on creating a great product that understood the user's search intent was the utility that they brought to the world. The utility they made was enough to attract attention from some of the biggest names in tech. It wasn't until two years later that they would finally incorporate AdWords into their search engine and monetize their traffic.

We see a lot of similarities when comparing those early Internet days with early non-fungible tokens (NFTs). The vast majority of NFTs have no utility beyond investment speculation—in much the same way that Ask Jeeves and Yahoo Search were simply joining in on the action of search engines with no real differentiation. And because we're in the early days of NFTs, these directionless projects can get a lot of attention, even though there's no use case for them. However, as time passes, we'll see a greater focus on NFTs with utility—tokenized projects solving a problem or creating something unique for users. Those projects that lack a use case will miss out on the real money to be made a few years from now.

Take, for example, the Bored Ape Yacht Club. The founders have created 10,000 Bored Ape NFTs that act as membership cards into the Internet Yacht Club. Right now, this membership card gives you access to a digital bathroom where you can take a "pen" and draw, write, or graffiti on the walls every 15 minutes. It sounds insignificant, but it's a unique experience. They've carved out this digital environment reserved only for the Bored Ape NFT owners. Yes, the Bored Apes are collectibles in essence. But it's the access and the utility that they provide that excites us for the future of this project.

Access might be the most significant use case of NFTs currently. In other words, to what does owning an NFT grant you access? We're surely going to see the utility of NFTs go way beyond this. Especially considering the wide variety and diversity of people getting into NFTs right now, there are so many exciting individuals with all types of ideas coming together to collaborate and create magical experiences.

Now is the time for experimentation, collaborating with others, and not working in a silo. This book is a product of two people experimenting with NFTs in their respective fields and starting a random conversation that ballooned into so much more.

QuHarrison Terry was working on selling the World-StarHipHop Chain NFT and creating liquidity for pop culture–focused NFTs. Matt Fortnow created the official Three Stooges NFTs and contemplated how iconic intellectual property could exist as NFTs.

Let's rewind the tape back to the early Internet 1.0 days: 1995. Matt practiced entertainment law in New York City when a few fraternity brothers from Carnegie Mellon University recruited him to start an Internet company. They founded Commissioner.com, the Web's first fantasy sports service, which they sold to CBS SportsLine in 1999. Always looking to develop uses for new technologies, Matt got heavily involved in blockchain in 2015, virtual reality/augmented reality (VR/AR) in 2016, and NFTs in 2020. It's actually through the VR/AR connection that he met QuHarrison.

QuHarrison recalls:

"I got a call one day from a friend who said I had to talk with this Matt Fortnow guy. This was at the early peak of NFT hype in March 2021, so I was used to talking with many people about a lot of NFT ideas every day. The conversation took on a life of its own and went on for a couple of hours. We were just riffing about how NFTs were all about sales and liquidity, the possibilities of tokenizing IP and revenue streams, and just having a fun time sharing ideas. By the end of the conversation, we were like, 'Yeah, we need to write a book on this.' And that's how a marketer and an attorney-turned entrepreneur came to write a book on NFTs. Literally a chance conversation around this shared culture of NFTs. And I think that's the beauty of this space right now. At the precipice of any new technology, it's prime for collaborations between people of different backgrounds."

It may feel like you're late to NFTs. But you're actually early in the grand scheme of things because we just haven't seen all the use cases of this technology yet. For reference, there were only about 130,000 active users on OpenSea, the largest NFT marketplace, in August 2021. With more than four billion people who have access to the Internet worldwide, we're nowhere near the exciting times of NFTs.

If Page and Brin thought they were late to the Internet in 1998, we wouldn't have the most effective and intuitive search engine that we have today. But they looked at the emerging Internet technologies around them and had a theory on how it could be done better. That's where we are at with NFTs today.

Take the information in *The NFT Handbook* as a starting point for your NFT journey. We'll take you through the history of NFTs to the basics of creating and collecting NFTs to marketing your NFTs, and much more. There are many people talking about NFTs and sharing their thoughts, their strategies, and their ideas. Use this book as a launchpad to go out and learn more about what interests you about NFTs.

Equipped with what you've learned in this book, start connecting with people in the NFT ecosystem. There are many NFT communities on Twitter, Clubhouse, Discord, Instagram, and other Internet destinations with people just like you who want to connect and learn from each other. At this stage in the lifespan of NFTs, it pays to communicate, experiment, and collaborate. Ultimately in the canon of NFTs, we don't know whether the current NFT projects we're seeing will be more akin to Infoseek (one of the earliest search engines, not around today) or Google (late to the game but created a superior product that stands even stronger today).

We've also created `TheNFThandbook.com` with extensive resources and links. Since the NFT space is ever evolving, the website will feature ongoing updated information.

As we dive in, your first question may be, "What are NFTs?"

2

What Are NFTs?

Even before you think about non-fungible tokens (NFTs), which in their most basic form are unique digital collectibles secured by the blockchain, you must understand how collectibles work. Perhaps the following eclectic Beanie Babies parable will clarify the erratic and eccentric psychology behind why we collect.

Why People Collect

Before NFTs, there were Beanie Babies...

From stamps to Civil War weapons to sneakers, people collect many different objects in various formats. So, it should come as no surprise that there is a market for collectibles in a digital form. Conceptually, it's confusing. But on the sheer basis of wanting to own a unique item that others do not have, digital collectibles vary little from their physical counterparts. Therefore, to understand why people collect NFTs, we'll draw a comparison to a physical collectible that took the world by storm in the 1990s: *Beanie Babies.*

From its inception in 1993, Ty Warner, the founder of Beanie Babies, built scarcity into his product. The plush toys were distributed in small quantities to small retailers, avoiding chain retailers and large orders altogether. Ty didn't want people to be able to find or buy every Beanie Baby they wanted.

The company kept the number of Beanie Babies in circulation secret. It "retired" the production of certain Beanie Babies to create more exclusivity. It intentionally let misprints and faulty Beanie Babies through the cracks, which would become extra rare editions of the toys.

Around the same time as the Beanie Babies' rise in the public consciousness, eBay emerged and positioned itself as the online marketplace for buying and selling collectibles worldwide. It was a synergistic relationship that ballooned the resale value of Beanie Babies and validated eBay as a valuable tool for speculators in all collectibles markets.

Those lucky enough to get their hands on one of the retired $5 plushies could, at minimum, see a two- or three-fold return by listing it on eBay. Some rarer misprints, such as the "Pinchers the Lobster" misprint as "Punchers the Lobster," yielded one collector more than $10,000.

The Beanie Babies craze was in full swing toward the end of the 1990s. Robberies and even murders ensued over the pursuit of the plush toys. For example, at a Hallmark store in West Virginia in 1999, a security guard was shot and killed when tensions were high due to a late shipment of Beanie Babies.

Sane adults searched far and wide for the chance to get a single life-changing Beanie Baby. One set of divorcees battled over who got the Beanie Babies collection, believing it was the most valuable asset that the two had to divvy up.

Then in 1997, McDonald's got in on the craze with Ty Inc. Together they launched the Teenie Beanies product line in McDonald's Happy Meals and proceeded to sell 100 million of the mini plush toys in just 10 days.

Magazines, such as *Mary Beth's Beanie World*, which sold 650,000 copies a month at its height, published entire spreads on Beanie Babies, discussing their value as a speculative investment, which, with the right strategy, could yield more than enough to send a kid to college.

Just when Beanie Babies seemed to be a collectible that would carry on for decades, it all came crashing down. Talk of their overvaluation sparked an avalanche of Beanie Babies hoarders to list their toys on eBay, causing a significant oversupply. In turn, the price of Beanie Babies plummeted.

Seemingly overnight, people's collections of presumed valuable Beanie Babies became nearly worthless. The story of Chris Robinson Sr.—the man who spent more than $100,000 on Beanie Babies for the speculative investment—became the symbol for the crushing defeat that this collectible market experienced.

The *Financial Times* aptly called Beanie Babies "the dot-com stock of the soccer mom world in the second half of the 1990s." We don't draw this comparison to say that NFTs are doomed to the same fate as Beanie Babies, that is, a collectible bubble bound to burst. Instead, Beanie Babies provide an excellent look into the dynamics of why people collect.

The same basic principle that drove people to collect Beanie Babies drives people to collect NFTs: *scarcity*. Although other factors drive collectors to collect, such as investment, speculation, emotional connection, the fear of missing out (FOMO), and "the thrill of the hunt," at the core of collecting is scarcity. No matter what we collect, we do so because there are a limited number of those things.

Could the NFT market crash? Anything is possible. But unlike Beanie Babies, NFTs provide real-world solutions to problems plaguing the art and collectibles markets, as we discuss in Chapter 3, "Why NFTs Have Value."

Now that we've addressed why people collect, whether it's physical or digital collectibles, let's dive into the topic at hand: NFTs.

What Exactly Are NFTs?

NFTs are generally known as a particular type of digital collectible, such as digital art from Beeple, a digital trading card from Rob Gronkowski, a short video from *Saturday Night Live*, a picture of fortune-telling Curly of The Three Stooges with an unlockable Curly-esque fortune, or one of the CryptoKitties. But what exactly are NFTs?

NFTs are unique items verified and secured by a blockchain, the same technology used for cryptocurrencies. An NFT provides authenticity of origin, ownership, uniqueness (scarcity), and permanence for any particular item. Let's break the term *non-fungible token* down a piece at a time.

Tokens

Let's start with the word *token*. According to Dictionary.com, one of the definitions of token is "a memento; souvenir; keepsake." Since NFTs are commonly known as digital collectibles, one might think the *token* in NFT is derived from this definition. Although it may apply (somewhat), the *token* in NFT is derived from something entirely different: the blockchain.

Some of you may be fretting, "Oh no, here comes the technical part. I just want to know what an NFT is." To understand completely what an NFT is, you need to learn a little about blockchain. We promise not to make it too complicated.

You've probably heard of Bitcoin and perhaps some other cryptocurrencies. According to Investopedia, a *cryptocurrency* is "a digital or virtual currency that is secured by cryptography." Just know that cryptocurrencies are digital currencies that exist on the Internet. You can buy and sell them for investment purposes, buy things with them, or even stake them (essentially lending them to earn interest).

Whenever someone transacts with a cryptocurrency, whether buying, selling, transferring, staking, or purchasing something with cryptocurrency, that transaction must be verified. The verification process determines whether the sender has the amount of cryptocurrency being sent. This is what keeps a cryptocurrency secure and reliable.

When cryptocurrency transactions are verified, for example, with Bitcoin, the verification is conducted on a *group* of transactions, not a single transaction. This batch of cryptocurrency transactions is known as a *block*. Each block has a certain storage capacity. After the block is filled and the transactions have been confirmed, the block of transactions is then appended to the previously verified block, creating an ever-growing chain of blocks: a *blockchain*. The process repeats, and the blockchain grows longer and longer (see Figure 2.1).

So, the blockchain of a cryptocurrency is a list of all transactions (every single one) of that currency, going all the way back to the beginning of that cryptocurrency.

Every time someone buys or sells Bitcoin, buys something with Bitcoin, exchanges Bitcoin, or transfers Bitcoin, that transaction is listed on the Bitcoin blockchain. The number of daily Bitcoin transactions reached around 400,000 in January 2021,

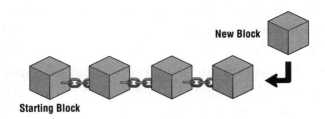

New Block

Starting Block

FIGURE 2.1   A blockchain

and Ethereum (the second largest cryptocurrency) was processed more than 1.1 million times per day (Statista.com). Think of a blockchain as an extremely long accounting ledger.

Coin vs. Token.   When speaking about certain cryptocurrencies, people often use the terms *coin* and *token* interchangeably. But that would be wrong because there is an important distinction.

Cryptocurrencies that are coins, such as Bitcoin, Litecoin, Dogecoin, and Ethereum, have their own respective blockchains. In contrast, tokens are cryptocurrencies that don't have their own blockchains. Instead, tokens utilize another coin's blockchain. For example, GameCredits (GAME) and SushiToken (SUSHI), among thousands of others, are tokens that use the Ethereum blockchain. Cryptocurrency tokens that exist on the Ethereum blockchain are also known as ERC20 tokens. *ERC20* is the Ethereum standard for creating cryptocurrency tokens.

GameCredits is an interesting case because it was initially a coin with its own blockchain. But to take advantage of the greater functionality that the Ethereum network offers, it switched to become an ERC20 token. So, now all GameCredits transactions (and all other ERC20 token transactions) are recorded on the Ethereum blockchain. This is the reason why Ethereum processes so many transactions a day.

So, the *token* in NFT is a cryptocurrency token. An NFT exists on a blockchain. Currently, most NFTs are created on and live on the Ethereum blockchain. Some NFTs are created on and exist on WAX, the Binance Smart Chain, and some other blockchains.

Non-fungible

So, we've got the token part down. Now let's turn to *non-fungible*. What does *fungible* mean? According to Dictionary.com, fungible is an adjective that means "(especially of goods) being of such nature or kind as to be freely exchangeable or replaceable, in whole or in part, for another of like nature or kind." Let's start with some examples.

Dollars are fungible. If we give you a five-dollar bill and you give us back five one-dollar bills, the exchange value is equal. It doesn't matter which dollar bills you gave us. Say that you had a stack of one-dollar bills. You could give us any five of them, and it wouldn't matter. You could even Venmo us $5. The fact is that dollars are entirely interchangeable.

Similarly, cryptocurrencies are fungible. If you send us a Bitcoin, we don't care what wallet it came from; a Bitcoin is a Bitcoin, just like a dollar is a dollar.

Even some goods or commodities (as the previous definition points out), such as barrels of oil, are considered fungible. It doesn't matter which barrels you send me. Any barrel of oil of the same grade would do.

Using the previous definition, it seems evident that non-fungible items can't be freely exchanged or replaced by similar items. For example, diamonds are non-fungible. Each diamond is unique in size, color, clarity, and cut. If you bought a particular diamond, it would not be easily interchangeable with another diamond.

Likewise, NFTs are non-fungible. Each NFT is unique. You cannot freely exchange or replace one NFT for another.

But what makes each NFT unique? After all, isn't it easy to download, copy, and share images from the Internet? Yes, but you can take a photo (or preferably create an image) and *mint* that image into a token that exists on a blockchain. We use the term *mint* like minting a physical coin.

When cryptocurrency coins and tokens are created, they are minted. Usually, millions or even billions of coins or tokens are mined or minted for a particular cryptocurrency. Generally, a cryptocurrency has a circulating supply, the number of coins or tokens already minted, and a max (maximum) supply, the total number of coins that can be minted. The max supply amount is baked into the original code that created the cryptocurrency and cannot be altered.

Contrast this with a fiat currency, such as the U.S. dollar, the supply of which can be continually inflated by printing more dollars. As more dollars are printed, the value of each dollar decreases, assuming that the demand for dollars remains the same. Thus, there is no max supply of dollars or other fiat currencies.

Bitcoin has a max supply of 21,000,000 coins, whereas Uniswap (UNI), an ERC20 token, for example, has a max supply of 1,000,000,000 tokens. Each NFT functions like a cryptocurrency, but NFTs have a max supply of 1. That's what makes NFTs unique and non-fungible; they cannot be freely exchanged with something of like kind because there is nothing of like kind. Think of an NFT like an original painting: there's only one. There can be copies of a painting or prints made, but there's only one original.

Even though we just said that an NFT has a max supply of 1, it is possible to mint an NFT with a supply greater than 1. For example, you could mint 100 "copies" of the same NFT. Technically, it's 1 NFT of 100 tokens. Each of the tokens could be

FIGURE 2.2   The Three Stooges "All Stooge Team" NFT, #19 of 30

exchangeable with the other tokens of the same NFT because they would be the same in every respect. Although these multi-token NFTs are considered NFTs, we would not technically refer to them as NFTs because they are fungible, albeit with a limited supply, but they are still fungible.

We need to distinguish between a multitoken NFT and a limited edition or series of NFTs of a particular design. For example, Rob Gronkowski issued four series of NFTs, the design of each series representing one of his football championships. Each series has 87 (being the number of his jersey) editions, and each NFT is individually marked 1/87, all the way up to 87/87. Similarly, The Three Stooges NFT series "All Stooge Team" is an edition of 30 individually marked NFTs. Figure 2.2 shows #19 in that series.

Albeit part of a series of 30, the NFT pictured in Figure 2.2 is a unique token with a supply of 1, which indeed makes it an NFT. Similarly, each of Gronk's NFTs are also unique NFTs.

One can make an analogy of such limited edition, individually marked NFTs to a series of prints of a painting that are also individually, sequentially marked. Whereas an analogy to the multitoken NFT could be a statue that is cast from a mold a limited number of times, and then the mold is broken. Each statue is an original, but also identical to the other statues from the mold. If each statue is sequentially marked, making each one unique, then this analogy would not be applicable in this case.

Edition numbers can have different valuations. With physical art prints, we generally assign the greatest value to the first edition of the print series, that is, edition 1 of 500. However, with NFTs, the driver of edition valuations can vary. For example, with the NBA Top Shots NFTs, it's common for the edition number that matches the player's jersey number in that specific NFT to be the most valuable edition. For LeBron James, edition #23 is often the most valuable, as is edition #77 with Luka Doncic or edition #11 with Kyrie Irving. Absent such an alternate value driver, edition 1 would likely achieve the highest value, like an art print.

Also, note that in the Rob Gronkowski and The Three Stooges NFT editions, each individually numbered NFT had to be minted separately. In the case of a multitoken NFT, all of the tokens of that NFT are created in one minting.

Types of NFTs

Generally, when you think of NFTs, you think of digital art and collectibles. These are the NFTs that are getting all of the press, especially with some of the lofty sales prices. But there are several other types of popular NFTs as well, and we'll cover them all in this section.

Digital Art and Collectibles

Digital art is a relatively new form of art, which had its origins in the 1950s. When computers became ubiquitous in the 1980s and 1990s, the medium exploded. Artists not only create their art with digital tools, such as a computer or smartphone, but the digital nature of the art is the medium itself. The art exists only in a digital format. Sure, an image could be printed out, but true digital art is intended to remain digital.

Digital collectibles are similar to digital art in that they are created digitally with the intent to remain in digital format. However, collectibles generally have a specific popular theme to which they pertain. Examples again would be the Rob Gronkowski digital trading card NFTs and The Three Stooges NFTs. Of course, a significant amount of artistic creativity went into these collectibles, and they are digital art pieces in their own right. For example, the Gronk NFTs were illustrated by artist Black Madre, with creative direction by Gronk, and some of The Three Stooges NFTs were created by artist Patrick Shea.

But in addition to digital art pieces, the collectible value is the NFT's association with Gronk or The Three Stooges. Digital collectibles are like actual collectibles, such as football cards, but exist only in digital format. Note that digital collectibles don't necessarily need to be digital art per se. A digital collectible could simply be a digitized photograph.

Digital art or collectibles could also be existing nondigital material with digital artistic elements added. For example, The Three Stooges NFT called "That's My Bitcoin!" is an existing photo with a digitally created Bitcoin digitally inserted (see Figure 2.3). This example happens to be obvious, given when the original photo was taken and the time that Bitcoin was created, but sometimes it's not so obvious.

FIGURE 2.3   The Three Stooges "That's My Bitcoin!" NFT

Generally, digital art or collectible NFTs can take on one of the following forms:

- Images
- Videos
- Gifs
- Audio
- 3D models
- Books and prose

Images.   Many NFTs are just still images, such as one of the CryptoPunks or a Beeple creation. Images can include any type of photograph, whether taken digitally or digitized (scanned) into a digital format. Of course, images could be original works of art or, as discussed earlier, a combination of the two. There is absolutely no motion in a still image.

With NFTs, there is no limit on the size of the image or its resolution, although some NFT marketplaces may limit the size of the file that you may mint. Generally, you would want to provide images in high resolution, which would allow them to be displayed on larger screens.

An image can be either raster (sometimes referred to as *bitmap*) images or a vector graphic. Raster images, such as .jpg and .png, files are more common. These are images that are made up of tiny squares (pixels). The issue with raster images is that if you enlarge them (scale them up), you will lose image quality. Vector graphics on the other hand, such as .svg files, use mathematical equations to draw lines and curves (vector paths) between various points. The advantage of this is that the image can be scaled up to any size without losing image quality. Vector graphics file sizes are generally smaller too. The advantage of raster images is that they allow for much more color depth, as each pixel can be one of millions of colors, so they're ideal for photographs.

Videos. Videos are another popular format for NFTs. NBA Top Shots NFTs, which contain highlight videos of moments in NBA history, has reached more than $500 million in sales. Not surprisingly, the LeBron James NFTs have been the most popular.

Videos are not limited to actual video footage, but also an increasingly popular form of digital art as well. For example, the Rob Gronkowski collectible cards are not static images, but videos. They were designed with a cool effect. Not only does the artwork of Gronk enter the cards from the side, but the cards also "flip over" to show you more detailed information on the back, such as the edition number and some of Rob Gronkowski's football-related stats.

Although most video formats don't repeat by nature, some sites, like OpenSea, will loop videos automatically. Because of this, the last frame of the video is often designed to line up with the first frame, creating a seamless loop. For example, one of the Sean Mendes NFTs features a rotating figure of a cartoon-like statue of Sean continuously rotating. In some cases with videos, the last frame does not line up with the first frame, and the image jerks back to the beginning. This can have a slightly jarring effect, which is why when creating videos or GIFs (discussed next), it's better to create a seamless loop.

However, when dealing with actual video footage that wasn't intended to loop seamlessly, the characters seem to jump back to their original positions. It's not necessarily bad, but a seamless loop, at least to us, is more aesthetically pleasing. An example of this would be The Three Stooges "Disorder in the Court" NFT, where Curly "soitenly" has an odd way of preparing himself for the witness stand. There's not too much that you can do when dealing with old video footage except try to find a short "scene" that ends close to where it starts. Figure 2.4 are the first and last frames of the "Disorder in the Court" NFT.

One can potentially overcome this effect by including a short introductory slide or transition at the beginning or end of the video.

FIGURE 2.4   First and last frames of The Three Stooges "Disorder in the Court" NFT

GIFs. A *.gif* is a specific type of file format often used for making short, simple videos that automatically repeat (or loop). GIF stands for Graphic Interchange Format, which also supports still images. In fact, GIFs were originally developed for still images, but since multiple images can be stored in one GIF file, GIFs became ideal for short videos or animations. Some people refer to GIFs of video or animation as animated GIFs. But to us (and most people), even though GIFs can be still images, calling a GIF an animated GIF is redundant. There's no reason to use the GIF file format unless it's animated.

The advantage of GIFs over standard video files is that they automatically repeat by nature; there's no need for a play button. On a site like OpenSea, a standard NFT video (such as in .mp4 format) will automatically play and repeat, but that's only on the NFT's page. If you go to the collections page, you'll see a preview (or thumbnail) image of the NFT, with a play button, and you will need to click the play button in order to play the video on the collection page. With a GIF, since the GIF format automatically repeats, you will see the video repeating on the preview page as well as on the NFT's page. There will be no play button on the GIF on the collections page. In fact, you will never see a play button on a GIF anywhere, because it automatically loops by nature.

There are some disadvantages to GIFs because they are an older technology. One disadvantage of GIFs is that they are limited to 256 colors. This may not be noticeable or a problem for most animations but would definitely be noticeable if you're converting a high-quality video to a GIF. If the video quality and resolution of the NFT are important, then a video file is preferred. Also note that GIFs have no audio.

GIF file sizes are also much larger than standard video files such as MP4. This is mainly because the compression algorithm for GIFs is less efficient. So, when creating GIFs, it may be necessary to reduce the dimensions of the images or video or reduce the frame rate (the number of frames, or images, per second). Reducing the length (in time) of the video would also help, which is why GIFs are usually short videos or animations, just a few or several seconds.

This leads us to the question of how to create GIFs. There's specific software for creating GIFs and other video software from which you can export your creation in GIF format. There are also online GIF converters that will convert most standard video files into GIFs. One must be cautious, though, when using online converters of any type because when you're uploading your creations to the Internet, you never really know where they might end up. If you do use one, make sure that it's one with a good reputation.

A final word on GIFs: they're great. They work really well as NFTs, but generally only for short animations, whether digital art or collectibles.

Audio.   Yes, you can make audio NFTs. Kings of Leon was the first popular band to release an album as an NFT, and it generated more than $2 million in sales. In addition to major artists, independent artists are finding audio NFTs, and other types of NFTs as well, as a great way not only to sell their music but also to energize and expand their fan base.

For NFTs, we suggest using a `.wav` audio file if available, rather than an `.mp3` file. `.wav` files are uncompressed, while `.mp3` files are compressed, which results in higher sound quality for `.wav` files.

In some NFT marketplaces, such as OpenSea, you'll need to include a preview image (or GIF) for the audio NFT. This could be album cover art or any other image or GIF.

3D Model.   A *3D model* is a three-dimensional representation of a specific real-world or conceptual object or artistic design. 3D models are integral to several industries, including virtual and augmented reality, video games, movies, architecture, and medical and other scientific imaging, to name a few. 3D modeling is gaining popularity with digital artists as well.

3D models can be viewed with virtual or augmented reality headsets. They can also be rendered on two-dimensional screens and rotated in all directions by "grabbing" the rendering with your computer mouse (or finger on a smartphone or tablet) and moving it, as well as having the ability to zoom in and zoom out. You can also print (make a physical model of) a 3D model with a 3D printer.

You can make an NFT of a 3D model at some marketplaces, such as OpenSea. The VeVe mobile app is a marketplace that specializes in selling 3D model NFTs.

Books and Prose.   NFT content can be just text, such as a poem, a short story, or even an entire book. I haven't seen too many NFT books or other prose examples, but there definitely are some out there. So, if you're looking for another avenue to monetize your writing, NFTs might be it.

In-Game Items

There are currently 2.81 billion video gamers worldwide, and the number is expected to grow to more than 3 billion by 2023. This is quite a significant percentage of the world's population.

In a multitude of popular games, such as *Counter-Strike: Global Offensive* (CS:GO) and *Dota 2*, in-game items, including weapons, armor, and skins (designs that go over your armor or other gear), are available for sale as in-game items. So, if you want to gear up quickly, instead of earning items in games, which could take many hours of gameplay, you can purchase a variety of gear instead. Lots of gamers want more firepower and other advantages in a game and don't want to wait. Game developers reap huge profits from these items, as they're just bits of computer code. According to the popular game *Gods Unchained*'s website, in 2019, players spent $87 billion on *in-game items*.

Players often accumulate multiple items throughout their gameplay experience with a particular game. At some point, that player will want to move on to a different game—the next fun experience. At first, players would be stuck with the in-game items they purchased (sometimes for relatively significant amounts). Then, in-game item marketplaces started popping up, where players could sell their no longer needed items to new players eager to gear up for the game and looking for reasonable prices. Also, some items could be rare and no longer available in the game. According to various reports, someone paid anywhere from $100,000 to $150,000 for a rare CS:GO skin.

The problem with "owning" these in-game items is that they are subject to the whims of the game developer. If the game's user base drops, the developer may stop supporting it, rendering your item useless. What if you paid a significant amount for a rare item, then the game developer creates thousands more of that item? What if you get banned from the game? Some games don't allow the selling of in-game items, and if found out, you will most likely get banned. Also, as with many industries, the in-game item secondary markets can be rife with scammers.

Some game developers have now taken to creating NFTs of in-game items. For example, *F1 Delta Time* is an Animoca Brands game where the in-game items are NFTs (see Figure 2.5). Players must have car, driver, and tyre (Brit spelling for "tire") NFTs to compete. NFTs for the game also include a driver's gear such as helmets, suits, shoes, and gloves, as well as enhancements for your car, such as front and rear wings, transmission, suspension, and brakes.

The NFTs contain each piece of equipment's properties and boosts, such as that specific part's effect on your car's acceleration,

FIGURE 2.5 F1 Delta Time "Intermediate Tyres" NFT selling on OpenSea

grip, and top speed. And because they're NFTs, the ownership and authenticity of the items are verified by the blockchain.

Digital Trading Cards

When you think of trading cards, you're probably thinking about baseball cards or other cards that come in a pack, maybe with a stick of bubble gum. At least that's what comes to mind.

Another type of popular trading cards are collectible *digital game trading cards* for popular games such as Magic: The Gathering. How popular is Magic: The Gathering? According to Wikipedia, there are more than 35 million players, and more than 20 billion Magic cards were produced between 2008 and 2016. These are actual physical cards, used in gameplay, which can represent different types of energy or spells. Magic cards are traded on exchanges and sites like eBay.

You may have heard of Mt. Gox, one of the first Bitcoin exchanges, infamous for having been hacked. It started out originally as a website for trading Magic: The Gathering cards. Mt. Gox stands for "Magic: The Gathering Online eXchange."

The next evolution in digital trading card games brought them online. One popular example is Hearthstone by Blizzard Entertainment. According to Wikipedia, by the end of 2018, Hearthstone amassed more than 100 million players. Technically, although Hearthstone is played with cards, similar to Magic: The Gathering, it's not a trading card game because the cards are not tradable. Despite players' requests, Blizzard didn't add this functionality. This may be why, or at least one of the reasons, Hearthstone's popularity has been tapering.

Thus, this is the reason for the rise of NFT trading cards, specifically digital collectible game cards in the vein of Magic: The Gathering and Hearthstone. One popular example is *Gods Unchained*, where cards you earn or buy are NFTs, minted on the Ethereum network. They can be used in gameplay, traded, and sold on NFT marketplaces. The fact that they're NFTs means that the player actually owns their cards, and they can dispose of them as they want. The *Gods Unchained* website boasts, "If you can't sell your items, you don't own them."

Digital Real Estate

Similar to in-game items, *digital real estate*, also known as virtual real estate, can be sold as NFTs. Digital real estate is somewhat of an oxymoron because it's not real. It exists only in a virtual environment. But for the purposes of the virtual environment, it is real estate in that it's land or structures on land and can have real-world value.

Virtual worlds, such as Decentraland, are online environments that simulate the real world in which multitudes of people explore the world and interact through their *avatars*, which are customized representations of the user. Like the settlers of old, people in the virtual world have a desire to purchase a nice plot in the virtual world and settle down. Or, as in the real world, speculators may buy up several plots with the hope of flipping them for a profit in the future.

According to Reuters, "Decentraland has seen more than $50 million in total sales, including land, avatars, usernames and wearables like virtual outfits. A patch of land measuring 41,216 virtual square metres sold for $572,000 on April 11, which the platform said was a record."

NFTs are a perfect way to sell and transfer virtual land, as the ownership and authenticity of the land is verified on a blockchain. The Sandbox is an example of a virtual world in which all assets and land are NFT-based. They have a built-in marketplace, but one of the advantages of NFTs is that they can be sold on any NFT marketplace, such as OpenSea. In fact, the Sandbox even has its own collection on OpenSea of virtual land.

Similar to how real estate deeds have a description of the property based on a survey, NFTs of digital land also specify the location of the land within the virtual world. Transfers of real estate deeds are usually recorded in the local county clerk's office. Transfers of digital land NFTs are recorded on a blockchain.

Is this digital real estate for real? Yes, it is, because virtual worlds are wildly popular. The game Fortnite has more than 350 million registered users alone. Although you can't purchase land yet in Fortnite, the Sandbox virtual world has sold more than 76,000 "LAND" NFTs, having an aggregate value of $20 million. As adoption of virtual reality grows, demand for virtual land will increase too, especially if at some point there's a *metaverse*, a vast collective shared virtual space akin to the Oasis in *Ready Player One*. No need to wait for that, though, when it comes to real-world dollars being spent. In March 2021, a virtual house NFT sold for more than $500,000.

Domain Names

The OpenSea NFT marketplace has an entire section for domain names. Blockchain domains make for great NFTs. But let's make an important distinction here: we're talking about blockchain domains, not the regular domain names you think of when browsing the Internet.

Every day we use domain names with extensions such as .com, .net, .org, .tv, and several other common extensions to access various websites across the Internet. These common domain extensions, also known as *top-level domains*, are ultimately managed and overseen by a centralized authority: the Internet Corporation for Assigned Names and Numbers (ICANN), which is a private nonprofit organization that sets the policy for the global Domain Name System (DNS) and keeps track of who owns which domain names.

Instead of being part of ICANN, ownership of blockchain domains is determined by the blockchain, just like ownership of cryptocurrencies and NFTs are determined by the blockchain. Similarly, blockchain domains are also held in a cryptocurrency wallet. We'll get more into cryptocurrency wallets in Chapter 6,

"Creating and Minting NFTs." In essence, a blockchain domain is a blockchain asset, which makes it an NFT.

Blockchain domain names have extensions such as `.crypto` and `.eth` and are not commonly used for accessing websites. Instead, they are used mainly for simplifying cryptocurrency payments. As we'll get more into in Chapter 6, cryptocurrency addresses are long streams of random numbers and letters. This address may also be referred to as your public address or public key, as opposed to your private key with which you secure your cryptocurrency wallet. We'll get more into that in Chapter 6.

A Bitcoin address usually has 34 characters, for example, `18ZW9AQGdsYcCUYrrp1NDrtjAnTnTX4zRG`. An Ethereum address has 42 characters, for example `0x969Bbaa8473180D39E1dB76b75bC89136d90BD84`. With a `.crypto` domain, you can associate the domain name with your crypto addresses. For example, suppose you had the domain name `example.crypto`. In that case, you could set it up so you could receive Bitcoin, Ethereum, or any other cryptocurrency at that domain name instead of the lengthy address. When someone asks for your address, you would just send them your domain name, and the cryptocurrency being sent will go to your associated cryptocurrency address. One drawback is that if someone sending cryptocurrency misspells your domain name, you won't receive it, and it may even end up in someone else's wallet.

Although not currently common, blockchain domains could also be the addresses of websites like regular TLD domains. The resolving of the domains would not go through the ICANN-controlled DNS, but through alternate routes. Such blockchain domain websites would not be subject to potential censorship by centralized authorities. Most browsers only support DNS domain names, but there are browser extensions that make it possible for the browser to resolve blockchain domains. In the (near?) future, a browser extension would not be necessary.

An advantage of a blockchain domain is that, as an NFT, you pay for it once, and it's yours. Registrars for regular TLD domains charge an annual renewal fee. If you don't pay the renewal fee for whatever reason, you'll lose your domain name. With a blockchain domain, there are no renewal fees—it's yours outright.

Buying and selling of regular TLD domain names has been going on for decades and has been a big business for speculators. Early Internet adopters who grabbed common word domains such as `hotels.com` have cashed in big time. Back in 2001, `hotels.com` sold for $11 million. More recently, in 2019 `voice.com` sold for $30 million.

Blockchain domains are currently in the early adoption phase and have yet to go mainstream like regular TLD domain names. Nevertheless, the NFT blockchain domain market has already started to heat up with $100,000 paid for the blockchain domain NFT `win.crytpo`. There are still some great opportunities to grab common word blockchain domains, which would likely increase in value as the adoption of blockchain domains grows. Of course, there are no guarantees of how long that may take, or if mass adoption will occur at all. That's why they're called speculators.

Event Tickets

We've all been to events where you had a physical ticket that you presented upon entry. Tickets have been increasingly going digital, though physical tickets are still widely used. Even digital tickets can be just a bar code on your device that you print out and present as a physical ticket. Several digital ticketing services, such as Eventbrite, make it easy for event organizers to sell tickets. However, problems still persist, especially for large events like concerts and sporting events.

Sometimes you can't make it to the event, and you may want to sell your tickets. There are also ticket scalpers who will buy up blocks of tickets with the intent to create scarcity and resell these tickets at a profit. Matt can recall walking around Yankee Stadium before a sold-out game with the Red Sox searching for a couple of tickets. As an experienced fan, he could spot a fake ticket that some shady character might be trying to pawn off as real. Luckily, he never got burned. But once when entering a Knicks playoff game at Madison Square Garden, the guys in front of him were "Re-jected," as Clyde Frazier used to say. They had purchased bogus tickets. According to a CNBC.com article in 2018, about 12 percent of people reported that they had bought a concert ticket online that turned out to be fake.

Aside from scams, the secondary ticket market has grown to $15 billion. This secondary market has been facilitated by sites like StubHub, a marketplace for sellers and buyers of tickets. StubHub verifies the tickets being sold, but the service charges significant fees. Plus, you may need to mail in tickets or receive your tickets by mail, or overnight courier if the event is imminent. More importantly, none of the profit from tickets sold in the secondary market goes to the event organizers, concert promoters, or performing artists.

Enter NFT tickets, which solves these problems.

First, with *NFT tickets*, you don't need a centralized organization to verify the validity of the tickets because, as discussed earlier, an NFT's authenticity is verified by the blockchain. Second, the NFT could programmatically provide that a certain percent of the profit generated from resales be automatically sent to the organization that created the tickets. Mark Cuban, owner of the Dallas Mavericks NBA team, a maverick himself when it comes to technology, is thinking about turning Mavericks tickets into NFTs. In a March 2019 CNBC.com article, he said, "We want to be able to find ways so that not only can our consumers, our fans, buy tickets and resell them, but we continue to make a royalty on them."

Tweets

You may have heard in the news in March 2021 that Jack Dorsey sold his first tweet as an NFT for $2.9 million. Who would have thought that you could make an NFT of a tweet? It goes to show that the possibilities with NFT content could be bigger than anticipated.

Aspects of NFTs

Every NFT is really a piece of programming code, which on the Ethereum blockchain is known as a *smart contract*. There are standards that dictate what should and can be included in an NFT's code. Non-fungible tokens have certain characteristics that set them apart from regular fungible tokens. As mentioned, fungible tokens on the Ethereum network are also known as ERC20 tokens. NFTs on the Ethereum network are ERC721 or ERC1155 tokens. These are different sets of standards that allow NFTs to have various functionalities and traits, as well as to allow marketplaces and wallets to work with any NFTs on the Ethereum network. Note that the Ethereum blockchain is currently by far the most popular blockchain for NFTs. There are several other NFT blockchains as well, including WAX, which stands for the World Asset eXchange. One of the major companies using WAX for NFTs is Topps, which has licenses for the collectible rights (both physical and digital) for a number of sports leagues, including Major League Baseball. Other NFT blockchains include FLOW, which features the NBA Top Shots NFTs, and the Binance Smart Chain. We'll go into detail about the various NFT marketplaces in Chapter 5, "NFT Marketplaces," and which blockchain each marketplace utilizes.

In addition to allowing non-fungible tokens to be owned and transferable, the standards discussed earlier allow NFTs to contain the following aspects:

- Name
- Main content
- Preview content
- Description
- Traits
- Unlockable content
- Ongoing royalty
- Supply

For all practical purposes, a name, piece of main content, and supply (which is usually one) are required. The description, unlockable content, and ongoing royalty are optional. Traits can be a key aspect of the main content of an NFT or actually be the main content of an NFT. Preview content may be required in certain circumstances. The different types and variations are discussed next.

Name

This is pretty straightforward. Every NFT, like every piece of art, has a *name*. Sometimes you'll see the edition number, like "(2/10)" or "17 of 25" at the end of the name. This would indicate that, in the former, the NFT is number 2 in an edition of 10, and in the latter, number 17 in an edition of 25.

Main Content

The *main content* of a non-fungible token is the content about which the NFT was created. You can also think of it as the particular purpose for which the NFT was created. For example, for

FIGURE 2.6 Image of a digital art NFT and a domain name NFT

a digital artwork NFT, as shown in Figure 2.6, the main content would be an image, video, GIF, or 3D model. The main content of a domain name NFT is the domain name, which is usually represented by an image and may contain particular traits.

Whereas the image in Figure 2.6 is the main content for the digital art NFT, the image is not the main content of the domain name NFT; it is just a visual representation of the main content.

For digital game trading cards, the main content of the NFT contains both an image (or GIF) and particular traits, such as the strength of the spell or other item that the image represents.

For digital land, the main content is the location of the land within that particular virtual world, and it is usually represented by an XY (X, Y) coordinate.

Where the visual is the main content of an NFT, such content can be in pretty much any file format. However, if you're creating an NFT on one of the several marketplaces, the allowable file format and size varies from marketplace to marketplace. If you're creating an NFT on OpenSea, for example, this content can be in any one of the following file formats: JPG (image), PNG (image), GIF, SVG (vector graphic), MP4 (video), WEBM (video), MP3 (audio), WAV (audio), OGG (audio), GLB (3D model), or GLTF (3D model). On OpenSea, the maximum allowable file size is 40 MB.

Preview Content

If the main content is not the image, such as is the case with an audio NFT, the main content can be represented by a piece of *preview content*, which would mostly be an image or a GIF. Such an image could be the album cover artwork or any other artwork, photo, or other image to represent the song. Note that programmatically, NFTs don't require a preview image. The purpose of the preview image is to make the NFT more visible and distinctive in marketplaces and collections, as opposed to a generic graphic of two musical notes, or nothing at all.

There is a clear distinction between a preview image and a thumbnail image. Thumbnails are reduced-size images or videos, which are generally used to represent NFTs when there are multiple NFTs presented on a particular page, such as in a marketplace or collection. Generally, clicking a thumbnail will take you to the NFT's detail page or to the full-size image or video that the thumbnail represents. If there's a play button on a video thumbnail and you click it, the video will play, rather than taking you to the NFT's detail page.

Description

This is also pretty straightforward. In addition to describing the NFT, *descriptions* can be used to indicate the edition number, describe what the unlockable content is, provide copyright or trademark notice, and mention other perks, if any, that the highest bidder will be awarded.

The following is the description of the Official Three Stooges "Crypto Moe" NFT:

> "The Stooges have gone 8 bit, which, if you think about it, is four times better than two-bit.

> "This super rare Crypto Moe NFT collectible is a unique one-of-a-kind number 1 in a series of 1. There ain't any others, and no others will be minted.

> "The highest bidder of this auction will also be awarded the opportunity to meet one of Moe's family members.

> "The Three Stooges® is a registered trademark of C3 Entertainment, Inc. The Three Stooges® characters, names, likenesses and all related indicia are trademarks and property of C3 Entertainment, Inc. © 2021 C3 Entertainment, Inc. All Rights Reserved."

Perks.   The description is also where additional perks, if any, are usually mentioned. *Perks* are additional items or experiences that the winning bidder will also be awarded. For example, the Rob Gronkowski "(1-of-1) GRONK Career Highlight Card" NFT had this perk in the description: "In addition to winning the Career Highlight NFT card, the highest bidder of this auction will be awarded the opportunity to meet Rob Gronkowski and attend one of his football games & win VIP All-Access Tickets to the next Gronk Beach. (2x tickets / mutually agreeable game in 2021 season)." We're not sure what Gronk Beach is, but it sounds like fun. The description also added, "Must be holding this NFT on April 30, 2021, to redeem this offer." So, if there are any special conditions to the perks, those should be mentioned as well.

Perks are great to include in an NFT and will obviously up the NFT's value. How awesome would it be to meet Gronk?

Well, someone thought it would be really awesome and bought the NFT for 229+ Ethereum, a value at the time of more than $433,000.

Physical Items.   An NFT's description can also tie the NFT to a physical asset. For example, the Slabs collection on OpenSea has the following description:

> ### Digital NFT Trading Cards backed by physical, graded assets, aka "Slabs"!
>
> "Collect and invest in tokenized physical sports and trading (TCG) cards. All tokens represent cards graded by reputable companies like PSA/BGS with distinct grades. (ie, a PSA 10 is distinct and separate from a BGS 9.5) Cards are stored securely in off-site locations like PWCC Vault and others. Build your digital collection and skip the shipping & storage hassles.
>
> "You may optionally redeem your NFT to receive a physical card. Full instructions are in the unlockable content. Redeemed tokens are destroyed, and the new owner is responsible for all shipping costs, fulfillment fees if applicable, and insurance. Visit our link for more details. NFTs with a serial # from the grading company will match the one in custody, but may not always be the exact card you receive. You will always receive the exact same grade by the same company."

Note that this Slabs description is not in any of the Slabs NFTs descriptions but in the description of the collection.

Similarly, a digital artist could put in the description of an NFT that the NFT owner is entitled to the original pen-on-paper drawing upon which the NFT artwork is based.

NFTs are an interesting and convenient means of "owning" a physical asset by owning the NFT without ever having to take possession of the physical asset. This type of use of an NFT is likely to gain some momentum, but an obvious question remains: What happens if the creator of the NFT does not deliver the asset when you redeem the NFT? In reality, you just own the NFT and a promise. Again, this goes against the value of a blockchain asset by requiring the trust of a third party.

Attributes

NFTs have the ability to contain certain attributes and properties. This is of particular importance when dealing with NFTs for in-game items and digital game trading cards for example. *Attributes* can be different properties or categories the NFT falls within as well as the powers or advantages (sometimes referred to as *boosts*) that the NFT provides and how much extra power or other advantage the NFT provides. For example, let's take a look at the attributes of an NFT of a pair of F1 Delta Time racing "Gloves," as shown in Figure 2.7.

The first area, labeled Properties, shows which categories the NFT falls within and what percent of NFTs are contained in that category. First, you can see that these gloves are in the Gear category, and that they have a Gear Type of Gloves. They are from the 2020 Season and are in the Rare Tier. These categories are set up by the game developer and may vary from game to game. Compare these categories to those shown in Figure 2.8.

As you can see, different property categories will be utilized by different games.

For the racing gloves NFT, the rarity level is 4 of 9. Though neither of the authors has played *F1 Delta Time*, we assume that 4 out of 9 is somewhat medium-rare. More important to the game would be the boosts. As you can see, the gloves provide a +395

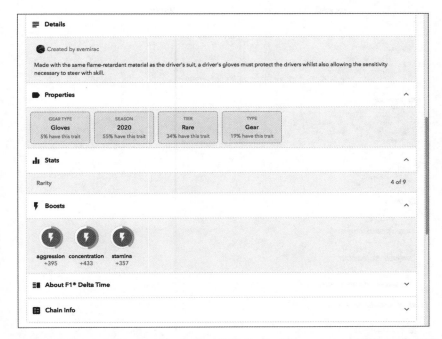

FIGURE 2.7 Attributes of a pair of F1 Delta Time racing "Gloves" NFT

boost for aggression, a +433 boost for concentration, and a +357 boost for stamina. The Sign of Avarice card has an Attack level of 3, a Health level of 3, and a Mana level of 4. Again, we haven't played Gods Unchained either, but from what we understand, Mana is the level of energy required to play the card.

The number of attributes or properties that an NFT can contain is theoretically limitless. It's up to the game developer, the NFT creator, and any display limits that may be imposed by a particular marketplace.

Unlockable Content

Unlockable content is cool. It's content that only the owner of the NFT can see or access. Unlockable content not only adds value because there's additional content included in the NFT, but it

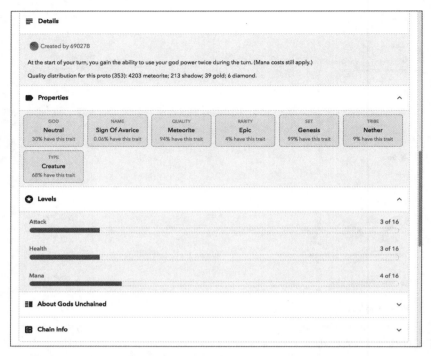

FIGURE 2.8 Attributes of a Gods Unchained NFT of "Sign of Avarice ID #73809"

also creates curiosity, which can add value as well. The NFT's description may describe what the unlockable content is, or it can be left as a complete surprise.

Unlockable content can be any kind of content. In addition to actual files (such as image or video), examples include contact information for redeeming physical items or other perks, login credentials for something (such as a website or online training program), a game activation key, a note from the NFT creator, or even your fortune as told by Curly from The Three Stooges, as in one of the Fortune Curly NFTs.

Note that on some marketplaces, such as OpenSea, the actual viewable unlockable content is only text. So, if you want to reveal some other type of content, such as image or video files, you will need to provide links to such files. Or you could provide an email address with instructions for them to email you and then email the files to them.

Ongoing Royalty

Another groundbreaking aspect of NFTs is that the creator can set an *ongoing royalty*. This means that every time the NFT is sold in the future, a certain percentage will go back to the original creator. Now artists and other NFT creators can earn from future sales of their creations without having to do anything more. The royalty amount will automatically be sent to the creator's wallet.

The creator chooses what percentage royalty they would like; 10 percent seems fair. If the royalty rate is too high, it's a disincentive for future sales. Note that when an NFT is offered for sale or auction on certain marketplaces, such as OpenSea, potential buyers are not able to see what the ongoing royalty is.

Also note that on OpenSea, the royalty is actually set when you create your collection, and it will apply to all NFTs that you create in that particular collection. Also, the creator is able to indicate the address to which the royalties will be sent, which can be different than (or the same as) the wallet address used to create the NFTs. We'll go into detail about creating collections in Chapter 6, "Creating and Minting NFTs."

Further note that if you create NFTs on a certain marketplace and set an ongoing royalty for your NFTs, the royalty might not be paid if the NFT is sold on a different marketplace.

Supply

As we discussed, the *supply* of an NFT is usually (and almost always) 1, which makes it unique and non-fungible. However, it

FIGURE 2.9   The Three Stooges "NFT Hucksters" NFT 5/30

is possible to have a supply greater than 1, each NFT being identical in all respects. Please note the distinction between supply and the number of editions of an NFT, for example, The Three Stooges "NFT Hucksters" NFT shown in Figure 2.9 is #5 in an edition of 30.

The supply of this particular NFT is 1. This number 5 of 30 NFT is unique. There is only one "NFT Hucksters" 5 of 30 NFT. However, there are 30 editions of the "NFT Hucksters" NFT. Each NFT in the series is distinctly numbered. So, the supply of each NFT is 1, although there are 30 editions of the NFT.

What's Really in an NFT?

Are all the aspects of an NFT together in one place on the blockchain? Not really. An NFT is actually a smart contract (programming code) based on the ERC721 standard (for Ethereum-based NFTs). All of the previous aspects of the NFT are designated in the smart contract. Other than the supply and ongoing royalty, the aspects of an NFT are contained in the smart contract's metadata. *Metadata* is data about other data. For example, the metadata for a digital game trading card NFT might look something like the following:

```
{
    "name": "Elven Wizard",
    "image": "storage.googleapis.com/game-image
/0x0d7b893b3wdd389cf022530ccd1743ac1db56e4e
/0127847.png",
    "description": "Common Alpha Edition
wizard of elven descent.",
    "attributes": [
        {
            "trait type": "Strength",
            "value": 16
        },
    {
            "trait type": "Dexterity",
            "value": 20
        },
    {
            "trait type": "Wisdom",
            "value": 19
        },
    {
            "trait type": "Constitution",
            "value": 15
        }
    ]
}
```

Note that the NFT's image is not in the smart contract, but rather it is stored elsewhere and referenced in the metadata. The main reason for this is because the blockchain would get bogged down with large image and video files if such files were stored on the blockchain. That's why it's extremely expensive to deploy smart contracts that include image and video files. It's even expensive to store the metadata on-chain. So, most projects also store the metadata off-chain, with a reference in the smart contract to the metadata's location.

There are two main solutions for storing metadata and files off-chain. The first is cloud storage solutions, such as Amazon AWS or Google Cloud, and the other is the InterPlanetary File System (IPFS). The IPFS is a decentralized peer-to-peer network of computers around the world (similar to a blockchain) where data and files are stored across multiple locations. Although these are the main solutions, the metadata and files can pretty much be stored anywhere on the Internet.

So, an NFT is technically a reference to data and files, and as we'll discuss in the next chapter, how these data and files are stored matters.

Extrinsic Elements of NFTs

In addition to the intrinsic aspects of NFTs discussed in this chapter, NFTs also have *extrinsic elements*. Every NFT, like every work of work, has a story behind it, which is tied to the NFT, whether stated or not.

One reason why you're reading this book is because you want to get involved with NFTs, likely start making your own, and eventually become successful at it. For many brands, influencers, companies, and other individuals wanting to get involved with NFTs, it can be tempting to look at the successful NFT sales and think that one can sell their own NFT simply on the strength of the value they've provided, the experiences they've created, or the history they've been a part of up to that point.

Sadly, this is not the case.

To achieve sustained long-term success, NFTs must have the following extrinsic elements:

- A compelling story of "why" you (the creator) are getting into the NFT market
- A reputation that you can translate to your NFTs
- Future assurance of lasting (or increasing) value of the NFTs

You may just want to dive in, make some NFTs, have fun, and see what happens. That's great, and you may hit the mark a few times. However, if you're serious about making it a long-term, life-changing endeavor, which is surely possible, strive for these extrinsic elements.

More than 14 years ago, Mike Winkelmann (aka Beeple) started a journey to create a piece of digital artwork from scratch every day. Today, this collection of *Everydays* stands at 5,100+ artworks strong.

As a computer scientist, Beeple had no background in art. He simply wanted to learn to draw and felt that publishing a work every day would build a following that helped keep him accountable to this feat.

Was his vision to eventually sell the first 5,000 artworks 13.5 years later in the form of an NFT for $69 million? Probably not. But it happened. Unpacking why this massive sale occurred, we can ascertain a few essential elements.

The Why

Simply, why do you want to make NFTs? There's no right or wrong answer. What's driving you? What's motivating you? Was there a particular inciting incident? How can you express your "why" in your NFTs and to your audience? Use your "why" to build a following.

Beeple's story of "why" was convincing. His entire brand was organically aligned to be an NFT artist. Up until his first NFT sale, Beeple took his art out of the digital medium and sold physical prints for at most $100. As a digitally native artist, it made perfect sense that his archive of digital art should be collected in the digital medium. Furthermore, the entire premise of *Everydays* was to showcase the growth of daily creative consistency. Therefore, owning one of his creations translated to owning a piece of Beeple's journey. What story will you tell that will make your NFT intriguing to collectors?

Reputation

Beeple's reputation was authentic. He spent 14 years giving to (and rarely taking from) his community. Beeple inspired others to better themselves, whether that meant learning Cinema 4D and OctaneRender (the software he used to create his mesmerizing art) or simply following in his steps and doing a task every day to improve. Reputation goes a long way. What's your reputation, and how does it align with your story of "why"?

Future Assurance

Buying a Beeple NFT came with a sense of future assurance. We know that Beeple will continue to create *Everydays* into the future, which reassures potential collectors that Beeple is in it for the long haul. He wouldn't be here today, gone tomorrow. How will you show the NFT market that you want to grow with the community?

When we juxtapose Beeple's immense success in NFTs against the failure of the Basquiat NFT, we learn even more about the essential extrinsic elements that we listed earlier.

Toward the end of April 2021, DayStrom listed an NFT version of Jean-Michel Basquiat's *Free Comb with Pagoda* piece. Along with owning the NFT, whoever won the auction would then be given the right to destroy the original physical Basquiat—wiping it entirely from the physical medium and leaving only the digital version. The theory behind this was that destroying the original would make the NFT more valuable.

After a couple of days (with no bids) the NFT was removed from sale due to a copyright dispute.

How is it that a computer scientist who created digital art in his free time could sell more than $75M worth of NFTs, but an art icon couldn't get a single bid?

While it's an intriguing story about the piece, they overlooked the fact that collectors might not have any interest in destroying a work of art by one of the most influential artists in American history. Furthermore, were they planning on listing all of Basquiat's work as NFTs? Would they all be given the chance of destroying the original? This strategy did not indicate future assurance.

Not every successful NFT drop incorporates the extrinsic elements listed earlier. And it's also by no means a comprehensive guide to selling your NFT, which we'll cover in Chapter 7, "Selling NFTs."

In January 2005, a man named Dave Roth would unintentionally make Internet history by taking a photograph of his 4-year-old daughter, Zoë, standing in front of a burning house mischievously looking back at the camera. The photo spread like wildfire and took on a life of its own as the "Disaster Girl" meme, one of the most recognizable memes in history. Sixteen years later, the original photograph was sold as an NFT for 180 ETH (or more than $700,000 at the time of this writing).

While we don't know why @3FMusic bought the NFT, we can assume that it was for its reputation and historical significance, rather than any future assurance or compelling story.

The value placed on NFTs might still seem like an enigma to you. Nothing more than random valuations pulled out of a hat. In the next chapter, we'll explore in greater detail why NFTs have value.

At the bare minimum, you should now understand why people collect, what are NFTs, the different types of NFTs, aspects of NFTs, and a few extrinsic elements that make for a compelling NFT.

Now, onto the value of NFTs.

3

Why NFTs Have Value

We've come to associate content on the Internet as "free." In fact, under the ad-based Internet model, we *expect* all content to be free. Tweets, memes, videos, articles—you name it—if it's not free, then the vast majority of us are just clicking away from it. For this reason, it's hard for most people to wrap their minds around purchasing something digital, such as a non-fungible token (NFT), which otherwise appears to be free: "Why would I want to buy something that anyone can view online, take a screen capture, and then claim 'ownership' of the digital result?"

The answer to this question is multifaceted, and we'll get into the reasons why throughout this chapter. However, just as we first covered why people collect in Chapter 2, "What Are NFTs?" we'd like to address an initial principle around "value" in order to create a baseline understanding of why NFTs have value.

Why Do Collectibles Have Value?

World War II recalibrated the importance of resources. Most of us are familiar with the nationwide rationing of sugar, meat, gasoline, tires, and paper. But did you know that copper was also on the list of resources in short supply?

Copper was essential to generator and motor windings, as well as radio circuitry and ammunition. With WWII taking place on land, air, and water, there were many more machines that needed copper wiring in order to operate. Not to mention, we could never create enough ammunition to fight the war.

Domestically, though, the United States wasn't producing nearly enough copper to satisfy the wartime needs. And can you guess who was one of the biggest consumers of copper at that time? The U.S. Mint.

In December 1942, Congress passed a bill authorizing the U.S. Mint to explore different metals for use in pennies. As a result, starting in 1943, the composition of pennies changed from 95 percent copper, 4 percent zinc, and 1 percent tin to almost entirely steel with a thin zinc coating to avoid rusting.

About 1.1 billion steel pennies later, the U.S. public pushed back against the change in appearance from brown to silver-colored pennies, and the lighter-weighted composition also confused vending machines. And so, the steel pennies ceased production in 1943, and we reverted to a 95 percent copper and 5 percent zinc penny composition (until 1982 when it was changed again to copper-plated zinc).

Within the one-year transition of materials, extra planchets (round metal disks ready to be stamped) of both copper and steel carried over into the following year. This resulted in 1943 copper pennies and 1944 steel pennies, which were supposed to be discontinued the year prior, but were produced anyway, most likely in error.

Approximately 40 copper pennies were created in 1943, and 35 steel pennies were made in 1944. When compared to the billion-plus pennies produced over those two years, these 75 errors were instantly rare.

In the process of contributing their part to the wartime effort, the U.S. Mint simultaneously created a rarified collectible for numismatists everywhere.

Fast-forward many decades, and estimates place the 1943 copper penny at somewhere between $150,000 to $200,000, and the 1944 steel penny somewhere between $75,000 and $110,000 (depending on their condition, of course).

However, as the saying always goes, art is worth whatever someone is willing to pay for it. This applies to collectibles as well.

In 2010, Bill Simpson, co-owner of the Texas Rangers, spent a record-breaking $1.7 million on a 1943-D copper penny and seven years later dropped another $1 million on a 1943-S copper penny (the "D" designates the Denver Mint, and the "S" designates the San Francisco Mint). These two purchases completed his collection of a 1943 copper penny from all three U.S. Mints in existence at the time (the other one being 1943-P, where the "P" stands for Philadelphia).

The fact that a penny, with a street value of 1 cent, can fetch a seven-figure price tag is absurd. But we can't think of a better metaphor for how collectibles appreciate and how they can represent a value far more than originally intended.

Simply because something is rare doesn't mean that it's valuable, though. There are many factors that affect the price of collectibles as follows:

Proof of Provenance Provenance relates to the origin of an item. When referring to collectibles, *provenance* is a record of ownership used as a guide to authenticity or quality. Proof of provenance, therefore, recognizes that a given collector's item is in fact what it claims to be. With respect to art, provenance is the documented chain of title from the current owner all the way back to the artist. When it comes to art and collectibles transactions, provenance can make or break a sale.

Historical Significance   The time period in which a collectible was created, or the historical story leading up to its creation, can impact the price of the collectible. The fact that WWII inadvertently caused the creation of the rare 1943 and 1944 pennies plays into the story of that coin. It adds to the complexity of why it happened, which is in stark contrast to the many other error coins that have been released from mints throughout history simply by mistake.

Sentiment   The emotional connection between collector and collectible cannot be downplayed either. And this sentimental connection can lead collectors to overpay for a collectible just because it means something significant to them.

Condition   Obviously, the condition of a collectible matters. Collectibles of all kinds are analyzed and graded for their wear and tear. When it comes to one-of-one, unique pieces, the condition doesn't play a significant role. However, when multiples of a collectible exist, as is the case in the wartime penny example, the better the condition the higher the value. This is why collectors go to great lengths to preserve the quality of their collections.

Collection Completion   Owning the entire set or variations of a collectible also plays into the price. For ultra-collectors like Bill Simpson, the thrill of the hunt takes over, and they want to have a complete collection. The rarer the collectible, the harder it is to complete the set. Therefore, acquiring an entire set of a collectible increases the value of the individual parts. In other words, it makes the collectibles more marketable.

It goes without saying that the value of collectibles may be an enigma to outsiders. Imagine trying to buy a million-dollar house with one of those rare pennies. You'd be laughed out of the room (by those who aren't aware of the penny's rareness).

Collectible value is rarely understood by people outside of that collectible's universe. But that's the point. Collectibles are largely driven upward in value because there are collectors. Supply and demand are the main function behind the value of collectibles. All of the other factors play into the story of the collectible, but if there's no demand, then there's really no value (at that point).

Another group of collectors who understand the principles that drive value are fine art collectors. And if there's one thing that all collectors must address, it's the piece's authenticity.

To understand NFTs and their value, let's first explore the problems afflicting the traditional art and collectibles worlds. Both fields throughout the years have been plagued by fakes, forgeries, other shenanigans, and lots of question marks.

The Problems with Traditional Art

A dirty little secret in the art world is that forgeries have for ages littered the art market, and the problem still exists today. According to a 2014 report by Switzerland's Fine Art Expert Institute (FAEI), 50 percent (that's right, 50 percent) of fine art in circulation on the market is forged or misattributed. Although that figure has been disputed, forgeries nonetheless continue to be discovered in private collections, galleries, and museums in a global market that saw more than $64 billion in sales in 2019.

Recent Forgery Scams

Art forgeries and fakes have been going on for millennia, yet the authentication methods have not changed at all. The following are just some of the recent art forgery scams that highlight the fallibility of the methods used to authenticate works of art.

The Old Masters Forgery Scam. A Frans Hals portrait, supposedly painted in the 17th century, was sold for $10 million in 2011. In 2016, it was found to have modern-day materials in the canvas, proving it a forgery. It's believed that this scandal could involve up to 25 Old Master paintings with a total value of $255 million.

The Knoedler Forgery Ring. Between 1994 and 2008, the Knoedler Gallery sold more than two dozen forgeries, with an aggregate value of $80 million, to unsuspecting buyers. A Long Island art dealer, together with her boyfriend and his brother, engaged an artist in Queens, New York, to create paintings in the styles of Jackson Pollock, Mark Rothko, and Robert Motherwell, among others. The ringleaders also created forged provenance (chain of title) documents.

Fake Giacometti Bronzes. A forger of Swiss artist Alberto Giacometti was finally busted in 2011 after selling more than 1,000 forged sculptures and fake bronzes to the tune of nearly $9 million over a 30-year span. Because recasting is easier than painting, the sculpture market is even shadier than the painting market. The scam continues to have repercussions today, as many of the forged sculptures are still on the market.

Fakes Sold on eBay. In 2016, a Michigan art dealer was caught using several aliases over a span of 10 years to sell dozens of forged artworks on eBay. The forged artists included Willem de Kooning, Franz Kline, and Joan Mitchell, among others. The forger also created fake receipts, bills of sale, and correspondence in order to provide provenance for the forged works. The Smithsonian may have been taken, as it has six works in its collection from this dealer.

Note that these are just a few of the most recent high-profile forgery scams. Going back a little further, between 1985 and 1995, Londoner John Myatt, often touted as one of the masters (of forgery), painted more than 200 forgeries of artists such as Chagall, Picasso, and Monet, which he had sold for multiple millions of pounds, duping the most prestigious galleries, collectors, and auction houses. Today, the art world is no better off when it comes to forgeries, and there doesn't appear to be any relief in sight.

Connoisseur Fallibility

In the art world, paintings and other works of art are authenticated by connoisseurs. These are experts who gander at a work attempting to sense the presence of the artist's hand. They then render a completely subjective opinion based upon their "expertise" and "experience." The obvious drawbacks of this system of authentication are that it's completely subjective—the so-called experts are fallible, have biases, and are potentially corruptible. When dealing with a painting that could have a value of tens or hundreds of millions of dollars, it's not that hard to get "fooled."

The high-end art world is also like a high school clique. If they don't want you in, you're going to have a tough time. Take, for example, a painting that then 73-year-old, foul-mouthed trucker Teri Horton bought at a thrift shop for $5. The 2006 documentary film *Who the #$&% Is Jackson Pollock?* (Picture-house, 2006) follows her journey to get the painting recognized by the art world as a Jackson Pollock. Not surprisingly, given the lack of provenance, the experts declared that the painting was an obvious forgery. Frankly, we'd be skeptical too. But then Teri Horton hired a forensics scientist who found a fingerprint on the back of the canvas that matched a fingerprint from a paint can at Jackson Pollock's studio. It also matched fingerprints found on other authentic Jackson Pollock paintings. On top of that, the composition of the paint on Teri's painting and paint from the floor of Jackson Pollock's studio matched identically under gas chromatograph analysis. Yet despite the forensic evidence, the "experts" to this day still insist that their original subjective conclusions are correct with one of them declaring that the painting just "doesn't sing like a Pollock."

It's shocking that many billions of dollars of value in the art world are relying on "experts." There's also no telling how many forgeries continue to lie in plain sight, once authenticated by connoisseurs.

Provenance Issues

The other factor utilized to authenticate works of art is their provenance, which as noted previously is a documented chain of title from the current owner all the way back to the artist. Often-times with art forgeries, the painting was "newly discovered" and has no, or little, provenance documentation. At other times, as in some of the previous examples, the provenance is completely fabricated with false documents.

Even more harrowing is the fact that scammers with forged paintings have been inserting fake provenances into the archives of storied institutions such as the Tate Gallery, the Victoria and Albert Museum, and the British Council, among others. How can any polluted archive be trusted with respect to any painting? It's not even known how widespread this practice is. Some archives may not even know if and to what extent they contain fake provenances. Additionally, some forgers have even printed fake catalogs and placed them in museum libraries.

It's unfathomable how disgraceful the art world has been, and continues to be, when it comes to authenticating works of art, especially when tens or hundreds of millions of dollars can be at stake. How can any work of art be trusted at this point?

The Problems with Collectibles and Memorabilia

The size of the global collectibles market is an estimated $370 billion. This covers a range of collectible items from sports cards and memorabilia to antiques, comic books, coins, stamps, and, of course, Beanie Babies, among several other types of collectibles. Similar to the art world, fakes and forgeries in the collectibles market are rampant. Up to 80 percent of antiques sold online are likely looted or fake. Twenty years ago (and perhaps still today) a potential 90 percent of sports memorabilia sold in the United States was fake. The FBI even had to crack down on counterfeit Beanie Babies.

Forgeries

All types of forgeries flood the collectibles market. The following examples are but a drop in the ocean.

Fake Signatures.   In the 1990s, in what was dubbed Operation Bullpen, the FBI infiltrated the nationwide memorabilia fraud market and cracked down on several forgery rings and individuals involved in forging signatures for all types of sports and celebrity memorabilia. Experts and cooperating subjects estimated that forged memorabilia comprised more than $100 million each year. The operation resulted in the following accomplishments:

- 63 charges and convictions
- Seizures exceeding $4.9 million

- 18 forgery rings dismantled
- More than $300,000 in restitution paid to more than 1,000 victims
- $15,253,000 in economic loss prevented in the seizure of tens of thousands of pieces of forged memorabilia through 75 search warrants and more than 100 undercover evidence purchases

One of the persons convicted in Operation Bullpen, Greg Marino, the subject of an ESPN film *The Counterfeiter*, is known as the world's greatest forger. From Babe Ruth to Mickey Mantle to Ty Cobb to Albert Einstein to Alfred Hitchcock, even Abraham Lincoln and many, many others, Greg Marino was the master. He would often forge hundreds of pieces of memorabilia a day. And that was just one forger of many.

Since Operation Bullpen, the industry has implemented authentication procedures whereby an "authenticator" would witness a signature and place an "authentication" sticker on the item or provide some other form of "authentication" certificate. Not surprisingly, fake authentication stickers and certificates have been popping up with forged items, somewhat akin to fake provenances for artworks.

I (Matt) have a friend, let's call him Barney, who used to go to baseball card conventions and collect signatures of the players who would ask $10 or so to sign a baseball. He got Ted Williams, Dom DiMaggio, Jim Rice, and Carl Yastrzemski for me. There's no "authentication" sticker, as none were available at the time, but I completely trust Barney; we grew up together.

Signature analysis experts could easily spot a crude forgery, but what about more masterful forgeries, like one by Greg Marino? We do feel that signature analysis is likely more scientific than art connoisseurship, but how can anyone really be sure that any signed collectible is authentic?

Altered and Counterfeit Cards. In addition to bagging multiple signature forgers, Operation Bullpen dismantled two counterfeiting card rings.

The most famous altered card incident is the subject of a book, *The Card: Collectors, Con Men, and the True Story of History's Most Desired Baseball Card* (William Morrow, 2007) by *New York Daily News* reporters Michael O'Keefe and Teri Thompson. The book focuses on one of the world's most expensive baseball cards, a 1909 T206 Honus Wagner. Only about 50 of such cards are known to exist, and most of them look like they've been around for a century. But one had sharp corners and appeared to have withstood the effects of time. It fetched a price of $2.8 million in 2007. It turns out that a sports memorabilia dealer had trimmed the edges to make the card appear as if it was pristinely preserved, and it worked . . . until he finally got caught.

Recently, altering of sports trading cards caught the attention of the FBI, who identified hundreds of cards sold for a combined $1.4 million, which were allegedly retouched or otherwise improperly modified by "card doctors."

The investigation also focused on Professional Sports Authenticator (PSA), the largest sports card grading company, on whom collectors rely to help determine the condition of cards, which has a major effect on a card's market value. PSA is currently a defendant in a class action lawsuit.

Fake Game-Worn Items. Fake game-worn sports jerseys and equipment is another area of rampant fraud in the collectibles market. In 2012, a Florida man was convicted on federal fraud charges for passing off replica sports jerseys as game-used. He would add patches and other identifiable marks so that they would look like professional athletes had worn them in games.

More recently, in 2018, New York Giants quarterback Eli Manning settled a civil lawsuit, which alleged that he was pawning off non-game-used equipment as game-used. Game-used helmets and jerseys have a distinctly higher value due to their scarcity and historical significance. Manning had entered into a deal with Steiner Sports, a well-known sports memorabilia company, who wanted Manning to provide two game-used helmets and jerseys. Manning then allegedly sent an email to the Giants equipment manager, asking him to send Steiner Sports "two helmets that can pass as game-used."

Degradation

Many collectibles are also subject to the travails of time, degrading over the years. There's even an entire industry of grading collectibles, particularly sports trading cards and comic books. Ultraviolet light, humidity, and even oxygen can have deleterious effects on collectibles of all kinds, not to mention handling of the collectible or the occasional accident. Although there are means to slow the aging process and provide some protection, a minute percentage of collectibles can be found in pristine condition.

As a collectible degrades, so does its value.

Digital Art Before NFTs

As discussed earlier, digital art is art that exists in a digital medium, such as an image or video. As the music industry frustratingly discovered, digital files can be copied and sent throughout cyberspace without any loss of quality. After a decade of figuring out what to do, the music industry developed digital rights management (DRM) techniques to slow the pervasive copying of songs in digital (mainly MP3) format. Streaming services such as Spotify were developed, as well as novel forms of royalties to monetize these new music distribution technologies.

Large stock photo, video, and clip art houses vigorously attempt to protect the work in their catalogs as well. They engage companies with software that crawls the web, searching for copies of images in their clients' catalogs. If you're a blogger or you posted a picture that you found on your website, you may have received a threatening email from one of these companies asking that you pay a license fee. How effective this is we're not sure, but some people probably pay, and others probably just remove the offending image.

But what about digital artists, the vast majority of whom are independent? They don't have the means to enforce their copyrights across the Internet. It's a gargantuan task for an individual. And how could you even sell, or rather, who would buy, a digital art piece if anyone can just copy and share it? We suppose that the artist could print it out and sell it. But then it's not digital art anymore, and you're dealing with the fraud-ridden art world. Out of the frying pan and into the fire.

The True Advantage of NFTs

NFTs solve the major problems plaguing traditional art and collectibles—authenticity and provenance—and they provide several other advantages as well.

Authenticity

Unlike the fine art world, NFTs don't require experts akin to dime-store psychics summoning the spirit of the artist to tell them whether he or she painted a particular piece. The authenticity of an NFT is verified by the blockchain.

As discussed, an NFT is a smart contract, and each smart contract, like a blockchain wallet, has its own address. In the case of an Ethereum-based NFT, the NFT's smart contract has a 42-character Ethereum address. Anyone can go to a block explorer, enter an NFT's address into the search bar, and easily find the NFT's smart contract. Additionally, the block explorer will show the address that originated the NFT. If the smart contract address matches the artist's (or other known creator's) address, the NFT is authentic. If it doesn't match, the NFT is not authentic and is not from the purported artist or another known creator. That's it. No uncertainty, no "experts," and no hocus pocus.

On marketplaces, such as OpenSea, you can also verify who created the NFT. On an NFT's page, just scroll down to the Trading History section and scroll all the way down in that section to see who created the NFT. If that is the verified name or address of the artist (or another known creator), then the NFT is authentic.

Provenance

NFTs have built-in provenance, a chain of title from the creator to the current owner. In fact, chain of title is the basis of blockchain verification, which applies to all cryptocurrencies.

As we discussed in Chapter 2, each transaction on the blockchain must be verified. Let's discuss in some detail how the validation process works.

A *blockchain* is a decentralized network, meaning that there is not one central authority or location of a blockchain (see Figure 3.1). There are multiple (thousands in some cases) copies of the blockchain (the list of all transactions) on different computers in different geographic locations worldwide.

Each copy of the blockchain is maintained by different people or groups. Each one of the computers in the network is referred to as a *node*. All nodes are constantly syncing with each

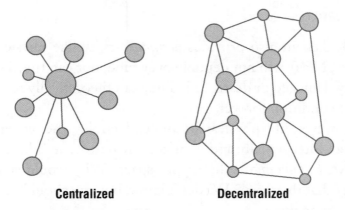

Centralized   **Decentralized**

FIGURE 3.1   A centralized versus decentralized system

other through a decentralized peer-to-peer network to maintain the integrity of the transaction data.

Miners or validators earn (or win) the right to validate transactions in a block. This is determined by the proof-of-work or proof-of-stake method, discussed later in the chapter. The validator must determine if the address sending the cryptocurrency actually has that amount of cryptocurrency to send. This is done by going up the chain: the sending address received the cryptocurrency from wallet B, which received it from wallet C, which received it from wallet D, and so forth, up to the latest verified block, which, in effect, validates the transaction all the way to the first block (the genesis block) of the blockchain.

Similarly, every owner (original, interim, and current) and transaction of an NFT is recorded on the blockchain. So, when you do a search of an NFT's address on a block explorer or check the trading history on a marketplace, you will see the NFT's creator, each successive owner, and the dates and amounts (in cryptocurrency) of each transaction. Such transactions are immutable (once they're confirmed on the blockchain), as is the nature of blockchain, providing an ironclad chain of title or provenance.

Permanence

The blockchain also provides *permanence*. Unlike physical collectibles, NFTs will not degrade over time, nor can they be accidentally damaged or destroyed. They can theoretically remain in pristine condition forever.

However, like physical art and collectibles, the owner of an NFT can intentionally and permanently destroy it. This process is known as *burning* in the crypto space. Why would someone burn art that they own? We don't know, but you should be aware that it can be done.

Scarcity

It would be nice if you could copy the Bitcoin in your wallet so that you would have double the amount of Bitcoin, wouldn't it? Well, obviously that can't be done. Bitcoin or any other cryptocurrency, or any currency for that matter, would be meaningless if anyone could just copy it. I (Matt) remember back when at the video arcade in the mall, a kid fed photocopied dollars into the change machine to get real quarters. The Secret Service came down on him hard. Creating counterfeit currency is a serious offense, as it should be, to maintain the currency's integrity.

Just as you can't copy Bitcoins, or any other cryptocurrency, you can't copy NFTs. After all, as we discussed, an NFT is a cryptocurrency, with a supply of 1. Thus, the scarcity of an NFT is ensured by the blockchain.

The scarcity, along with the authenticity of NFTs, makes it possible for artists to sell digital artwork without having to worry about unauthorized or fraudulent originals. It opens up an entire new market for digital artists and digital collectible creators—a market that never existed before—and one that is generating millions of dollars.

Ongoing Royalty for Creators

When a painter sells a painting, all the painter gets is the amount of money the painting sold for. When that painting is later sold to the next buyer, possibly for 10 times, 100 times, or even more, than the amount of the original sale, the artist receives no part of that secondary sale or any sales thereafter. There is no continuing royalty to a painter or other means for a painter to profit from the increased value of his or her work (other than to paint new paintings).

In addition to creating a whole new market for digital art and collectibles, NFTs can contain a continuing royalty, so artists and other creators can also share in future sales of their art. And artists don't need to invoice for it, track down the purchaser, go through a third party, or wait six months to receive it. The royalty is automatically sent to the artist's cryptocurrency wallet.

Note that ongoing royalties are guaranteed only if the NFT is sold on the same marketplace on which it was created. The ongoing royalty may not be paid if the NFT is sold on a different marketplace.

Advantages of a Decentralized System

NFTs, with their foundation on blockchain technology, benefit from the advantages inherent in a decentralized system.

No Single Point of Failure. Centralized transaction systems consist of a database and verification process that runs through one single location or central authority. For example, even though banks have several locations, they are centralized systems. A bank controls its own database and verifies all transactions in and out of the accounts held at the bank.

The problem with a centralized system occurs when there is a breach or hack. In such a case, the hacker is able to gain access to all of the records in the database and either steal sensitive data or even potentially alter data records. For example, in 2019, someone hacked into the Capital One database and obtained the personal data of more than 100 million people. The main problem here is that there was only one place that the hacker needed to attack to get into the database.

With a decentralized system, there isn't one point of failure that will allow an attacker access to alter the database. If an attacker is able to access one of the Bitcoin nodes and attempts to alter previous transactions or add new fake transactions to the blockchain, the other nodes will recognize these as aberrant, and they will be rejected by the remainder of the network.

No Single Controlling Authority. With a single controlling authority, again such as a bank, the bank (subject to certain government regulations) has full control of the database and how it's managed. Additionally, the bank has full control (once again, subject to certain government regulations) of how it conducts transactions. For example, you may have a check that you deposit put on hold for a period of time. The bank determines the length of the hold, and it can even extend that hold. Good luck trying to get those funds sooner.

As mentioned, with a decentralized system, no centralized authority controls it. In addition to all transactions being verified and processed in the same manner, you are not subject to the vagaries and whims of a controlling authority. More importantly, without a controlling authority, you actually have 100 percent total control of your funds. Only you, and no one else, can do anything with your funds (assuming that you have securely protected your password and private key, so your wallet does not get hacked).

Trustless Transactions.   In the "old days," transactions were conducted in person by barter—I will exchange these goods with you for those goods. We really don't need to trust each other, as it's a simultaneous exchange, and we each have a chance to inspect the other's goods prior to the exchange.

Later, when currency was developed, trust entered the picture. When purchasing goods with currency, the exchange is pretty much the same. I give you cash (or whatever is the pertinent currency) for goods. Now the seller has to be concerned that the currency is real (not counterfeit), that it has value, and that it will maintain its value (at least until the time the seller uses it to purchase some other goods or service).

Regarding whether the currency is real, the seller needs to trust me. To a greater extent, however, the seller must have the ability to detect whether the currency is counterfeit, as well as trust the government or other authority to enforce the counterfeiting laws vigorously in order to discourage attempts to pass counterfeit currency. Thus enters a third party into the transaction as far as trust is concerned: the governing body.

As commerce increased, people began transacting remotely, which required one or more trusted intermediaries to make payments. At first, it was a courier who would personally deliver funds. Now we have an advanced banking system. For example, if you wrote a check and mailed it to me, I would present it to my bank, which would then present it to your bank to see if the funds in your account are sufficient to cover the check. If yes, the funds would be sent from your bank to my bank, which would then credit my account. Obviously, in this scenario, the banks are acting as trusted intermediaries.

Now let's say that you are purchasing something online. The trusted intermediaries would be your credit card company, the seller's merchant bank (the bank that processes credit card transactions), and the seller's bank.

The problem with trusted intermediaries is that sometimes that trust is betrayed either intentionally or unintentionally. How trustworthy are these trusted intermediaries? Let's use banks again as an example.

Aside from all of the fees and charges, banks are capable of making errors. Such errors include processing errors resulting in an incorrect amount of funds in your account, transactions you didn't authorize, and additional fees or charges that should not have been charged.

If you've ever played the game Monopoly, you may recall the Community Chest card "Bank Error in Your Favor. Collect $200." That's great! If this happens to you in real life, however, and you spend it, you could "Go Directly to Jail." Seriously. If the bank error is not in your favor, you have only a certain time within which to notify the bank about it, and good luck trying to get it corrected without a major headache.

And then there's the Wells Fargo scandal in 2016, where bank executives put pressure on their employees to increase sales and revenue to meet aggressive quotas. These Wells Fargo employees then intentionally created millions of new accounts for customers without their knowledge or consent, resulting in new fees to these customers for something they never initiated or wanted.

How safe is your money in the bank? Under a fractional reserve banking system, banks can loan out a vast majority of their depositors' funds, keeping only a small fraction to cover customer withdrawals. This generally works, until multiple customers want to withdraw their funds simultaneously, causing a bank run. To prevent this, you may be restricted in the amount and frequency of withdrawals.

We often hear the phrase "too big to fail" when it comes to the big banks, but that's only because the government bailed them out. There could certainly be another financial crisis like we had in the United States in 2008. Will the banks still be too big to fail? If not, luckily the Federal Deposit Insurance Corporation (FDIC) should provide you up to $250,000 in coverage. How long it may take to receive your funds, we do not know. If you have an amount greater than $250,000 in the bank, good luck with that. The amount that you have on deposit in excess of FDIC coverage may be subject to *bail-ins*. Instead of receiving a government bailout, a bank may use; that is, take your money to keep itself afloat. This actually happened in Cypress in 2013. Uninsured depositors in the Bank of Cypress lost a substantial portion of their deposited funds.

The funds in your bank account can also be subject to liens and attachments and can be frozen or even seized. Banks can freeze your account even if you've done nothing wrong, just by declaring that your banking activity is "suspicious."

Given this, how much control do you really have over your funds? Look, we're not here to pooh-pooh the banks, which provide valuable services and keep our economy in motion. We're merely pointing out the issues relevant to centralized systems.

Now imagine remote transactions without the need for intermediaries. I can send currency on a blockchain directly to you. I don't have to trust you, you don't have to trust me, and more importantly, we don't have to trust or even deal with an intermediary. It is true that miners and validators must process blockchain transactions, but the processing is done programmatically in accordance with the rules and protocols set out in the blockchain's particular software, without human intervention. It may not seem like a big deal on the face of it, but sending funds with no courier, no bank, or no intermediary is quite a breakthrough.

Additionally, you are in full control of the funds that you hold on the blockchain in your blockchain wallet. They are not subject to onerous rules; do not incur fees; are not subject to potential error (unless it's your own human error); are 100 percent available (not subject to fractional reserve limitations or bank runs); cannot be subject to involuntary liens, other encumbrances, or seizure; and can't be subjected to bail-ins. As long as you are in full control of your wallet and you secure your private key, the funds are 100 percent yours. In Chapter 6, "Creating and Minting NFTs," we'll go into how to obtain and secure a cryptocurrency wallet.

One caveat to the foregoing is that if you want to have 100 percent control of your cryptocurrencies and other crypto assets, such as NFTs, they must be held in an independent wallet, not a wallet on a cryptocurrency exchange. For example, if your Ethereum is in your Coinbase wallet, it's not unlike having money in a bank. Another caveat is that crypto may be subject to government regulation, or it may even be banned. Many countries have instituted bans on various types of cryptocurrency transactions, such as China and Turkey, or have even completely banned it, such as in Bolivia and Nepal.

Speed.   Let's say someone in Italy wanted to send money to someone in the United States. They could mail a check, which would take some time, and of course there would be the time (probably days or even weeks) it would take for the check to clear. Alternatively, a much quicker method would be to use a bank wire sent through the Society for Worldwide Interbank Financial Telecommunications (SWIFT) system, which is a network of more than 11,000 banks and financial institutions around the world. On average, international wire transfers take two or more business days to complete. Since it's all electronic, why? Is the money taking a cruise across the Atlantic? On top of this, you're going to be hit with a sizable international wire transfer fee.

Instead, the person in Italy can send cryptocurrency to the person in the United States virtually instantaneously. The exact amount of time can vary depending on several factors, such as the actual cryptocurrency being used, network congestion (due to transaction volume), and in some cases, such as Ethereum, the "gas" fee you pay. We'll go more into gas fees later in this chapter.

Generally, a cryptocurrency transaction will take between a few seconds and several minutes, although it may take longer for some receiving entities to consider a transaction final. For example, Coinbase requires three confirmations before considering a Bitcoin transaction final. Confirmations are the number of blocks added to the blockchain after the transaction was initiated. The more blocks that are added, the more secure the transaction. Since Bitcoin blocks are added to the blockchain around every 10 minutes, a Bitcoin transaction sent to Coinbase will be pending for about half an hour.

Cost. Transaction costs for blockchain transactions are also (most likely) going to be less than an international wire transfer fee. Litecoin, a coin based on Bitcoin technology, has very low fees. On the other hand, Ethereum gas fees have been rising lately and can be excessive at times. This is a consequence of the increasing popularity and use of Ethereum (not in small part due to NFTs). The more transactions that need to be processed, the higher the demand and the higher the gas fee. Ethereum gas fees and other cryptocurrency network fees go to the validators—the ones who run the validator nodes that process transactions.

Anonymity. Many people tout blockchain as providing anonymity. Because you transact on the blockchain with your address and not your name or other identifying information, it would seem that you're anonymous. But is this really the case? Blockchains are public ledgers. Anyone can see any transaction or the holdings of any particular address. For example, if it's an Ethereum address, someone could see all of the different tokens that you're holding at that address, the amount of each token, when particular amounts of these tokens were received by or sent from that address, and in what amounts. Note that your cryptocurrency addresses are contained within a cryptocurrency wallet, which is an app that allows you to securely store, send, and receive cryptocurrency and NFTs. We'll go more into wallets, and even guide you on how to create one, in Chapter 6.

Searching transactions and addresses can easily be done by means of a blockchain explorer, often just referred to as a *block explorer*, a website where you can search particular transactions and addresses, as well as view all kinds of current data pertaining to the blockchain. For example, for the Ethereum blockchain, there's Etherscan (`etherscan.io`) and Ethplorer (`ethplorer.io`). Just enter an address or transaction hash (ID) into the search bar. So, if someone knows that a particular address is your address, then they can know what you're holding and what transactions you've made, but just for that particular address.

If you purchase cryptocurrency on an exchange, such as Coinbase, the exchange knows who you are. Any transactions originating from the exchange can be traced back to you, including further transactions that you make. For example, if you buy ETH on Coinbase, send it to your MetaMask wallet, convert it to WETH, and then buy an NFT on OpenSea, all of these transactions can be traced back to your original purchase on Coinbase. Then, Coinbase (and any party with whom Coinbase shared such information, for example, the government) would know that it's you who made all of these transactions and who owns that NFT. Not particularly anonymous, is it? Now there are ways to become more anonymous on the blockchain, but they are beyond the scope of this book. By the way, don't worry if the previous process completely baffled you; we'll go over it in detail in Chapter 7, "Selling NFTs."

Limits on Inflation. A country's government, in conjunction with their central bank, is responsible for maintaining the value of the currency, whether the currency is backed by (exchangeable for) gold, silver, or other commodity or, as in the case of the U.S. dollar, the full faith and credit of the U.S. government. The U.S. dollar is a fiat currency, meaning that it is not backed by a commodity or precious metal. As with any fiat currency, the supply can be continuously increased (by printing more money), thus reducing the value of the dollar and, therefore, causing inflation. Throughout history, there are also examples of hyperinflation due to the excessive printing of money, such as in the Weimar Republic in Germany and in Zimbabwe, rendering the currency virtually (or completely) worthless (see Figure 3.2).

In contrast to fiat currency, the supply of most cryptocurrencies is limited. Such a limit is inscribed in the initial programming code under which the cryptocurrency was created and cannot be altered. For example, the maximum supply of Bitcoin is 21,000,000. Once that amount has been reached, no more will be minted. As of the time of this writing, the current supply of Bitcoin is approximately 18.69 million. Each time a miner successfully completes a block, they get a reward, known as a *block*

FIGURE 3.2 Zimbabwe 100 trillion-dollar bill

reward, which is currently 6.25 bitcoins (BTC). Every 210,000 blocks, approximately every four years, the block reward is cut in half. Therefore, it is estimated that Bitcoin won't reach the maximum supply until the year 2140.

As mentioned, not all cryptocurrencies have a maximum supply. One example is Ethereum (ETH), the second most popular cryptocurrency. Currently, for every block, only 2 ETH are added to the circulating supply, which as of this writing is approximately 115.6 million. Given the rising demand for Ethereum, especially in connection with NFTs and other uses, any inflationary effects are minimal. The same goes for other cryptocurrencies that have not reached their maximum supply. Of course, once those cryptocurrencies achieve maximum supply, inflation will henceforth be zero. The main takeaway is that the value of a cryptocurrency can't be inflated away by the fiat of a governing body.

As discussed, NFTs, each technically being its own cryptocurrency, have a supply of 1, which is also their maximum supply. Note that, as mentioned earlier, it's possible for an NFT to have a supply of greater than 1.

NFTs Aren't Perfect

Given all of the advantages of NFTs over traditional artwork, collectibles, and other assets, NFTs are here to stay. NFTs provide an excellent medium for verifying authenticity and ownership, as well as the other functionality that we discussed. However, although NFTs may be touted by some as the perfect solution, in reality, NFTs are not perfect. They have several drawbacks that need to be addressed.

Gas Fees

When we talk about gas fees with respect to NFTs, we're not talking about the price at the pump when you fill your car. We're talking about transaction fees on the Ethereum network, which are known as *gas fees*, or simply gas. Not unlike the gas at the pump, gas fees have risen recently and are starting to get out of control and become a deterrent.

Gas fees go to the miners (validators) who process transactions on the Ethereum network. The amount of gas required for a certain transaction is based on two main factors. First, gas is based on the type of transaction. More precisely, the gas fee is based on the amount of computational power required to execute the operation. If it's a simple transfer of cryptocurrency, such as ETH, another token, or an NFT from one wallet to the next, the gas fee will be lower. If you're deploying a lengthy smart contract to the network, the gas fee will be significantly higher.

The second factor affecting the gas fee is network volume (sometimes referred to as *congestion*). The higher the volume, the more demand is created, which drives up the price of gas. Think of it like surge pricing on the Uber app during busy times. Due to a resurgence in crypto, in no small part because of the growing interest in NFTs, the number of transactions on the Ethereum network has been rising, along with Ethereum's popularity and price. For now, it seems that the old days of cheap gas are over.

Although rising, the volume on the Ethereum network is not continuously rising at a steady pace. The volume on the network fluctuates minute by minute, second by second, so the gas price is constantly in flux. One day the gas price for a particular transaction may be $30, while just a day later it could be $60, or more.

You may have an option, depending on from where you're originating the transaction, to choose a level of gas. For example, if you're sending crypto from a MetaMask wallet (we'll get more into this in Chapter 7), you can choose a level of gas corresponding to the desired speed of the transaction: Slow, Average, or Fast (see Figure 3.3). Note that for any given type of transaction, the miners are going to prioritize the transactions depending on their

Transaction Fee:	Slow	Average	Fast
	0.00794 ETH	0.00861 ETH	0.00905 ETH
	$32.93	$35.72	$37.55

FIGURE 3.3 Choice of gas fee presented in the MetaMask wallet

respective gas fees. If you select Slow, you could be waiting for hours.

Even though you may be able to make a selection, there are no guarantees on how long the transaction will take. If you select Fast, the transaction will most likely occur relatively instantaneously. If you select Average, the transaction will usually take a few to several minutes. However, gas prices may have gone up between the time you initiated the transaction and the time you confirm it. In such a case, the Average gas selected will be low and may take longer than expected—potentially a lot longer.

Hopefully soon, high gas fees will be a thing of the past. The Ethereum network is currently undergoing an upgrade, called Eth2 (or Eth 2.0). One result of this upgrade will greatly reduce gas fees, among other improvements. From the Ethereum.org website:

> "Eth2 refers to a set of interconnected upgrades that will make Ethereum more scalable, more secure, and more sustainable. These upgrades are being built by multiple teams from across the Ethereum ecosystem."

Other Blockchains.   Keep in mind that Ethereum isn't the only blockchain that supports NFTs. As mentioned earlier, other popular blockchains that feature NFTs are WAX, FLOW, Tron, and the Binance Smart Chain, among others. These blockchains have considerably lower transaction fees compared to Ethereum's gas fees, which is why they're growing in popularity.

The reason why these other chains have lower transaction fees is because they use a less resource-intensive method for determining who validates transactions. Blockchains such as Ethereum and Bitcoin use *proof of work*, which means that miners race to solve complex cryptographic puzzles (hence the name *cryptocurrency*). The miner who solves it wins the opportunity to validate the latest block of transactions and earn the block reward. Trying to solve these puzzles requires massive amounts of processing power (known as *hash power*), so the more hash power you have, the higher your chances are of solving the puzzle. Also, the difficulty of these puzzles increases as the total amount of hash power on the network increases, requiring even more hash power to solve. The reason why the difficulty increases is to maintain a time period between blocks of approximately 10 minutes.

The other blockchains mentioned earlier use *proof of stake* to determine who validates the blocks. Basically, the more of a certain coin a validator owns, WAX for example, the higher the chance the validator has of being chosen to validate a block. Since there are no cryptographic puzzles to solve, there's no need for wasted processing power, and thus the fees are significantly lower. As part of Eth2 discussed earlier, Ethereum plans to change to proof of stake, which would drastically lower transaction fees.

Sidechains. Another way to reduce gas fees is through the use of a *sidechain*, which is a separate secondary blockchain that's connected to the main blockchain. A sidechain allows tokens to be used on the secondary blockchain (one with little or no transaction fees), with the ability to move tokens back to the main blockchain when necessary. For example, at a particular NFT marketplace, you could mint multiple NFTs gas-free on a sidechain and only pay gas when the NFTs are sent to the Ethereum blockchain when you sell or transfer an NFT.

So, although gas fees may be an issue at present, there are measures in place to reduce gas fees, and proof-of-stake blockchains have significantly lower fees. When Ethereum switches to proof of stake, high gas fees may be a thing of the past.

Content Storage

Say you bought a digital art NFT that you love. The NFT's main content, the reason why you bought the NFT, is a really cool abstract video. The blockchain confirms that the NFT was created by the artist and that you now own it. But where exactly is your NFT's content? And more importantly, how safe is it?

We talked earlier about how the NFT is on the blockchain, but its content is not. The NFT is permanent so long as the blockchain continues to exist, but its content may not be. We touched on the two main solutions for off-chain storage of NFT content: a trusted cloud storage provider and the IPFS.

The IPFS is the preferred storage solution because it is decentralized; content is stored across multiple locations. So long as the network continues to be supported (and there are all indications that it will be), the content should be safe. Other decentralized storage solutions, such as Arweave, have also come to the scene.

Trusted cloud storage providers, such as AWS and Google Cloud, are also exceptional solutions. However, the content will be hosted only so long as the organization paying the cloud storage fees continues to do so. If the NFT was minted on one of the major marketplaces, this probably won't be an issue, but you never know. For whatever reason, the marketplace could go belly-up. It could happen—then what would become of your NFT's content?

Someone, an individual artist, for example, could also mint an NFT on their own (not on a marketplace) and store the NFT's content on a private server. If that server goes offline permanently, your NFT content is toast.

These scenarios go against one of the major advantages of blockchains discussed earlier—no need for trusted third parties. That's in essence the whole foundation upon which blockchain was invented—to provide trustless peer-to-peer transactions. Because an NFT's content does not reside on the blockchain and a third party must be relied upon to store and preserve its content (often the main content), NFTs are not true blockchain assets. Decentralized solutions such as the IPFS are most akin to blockchains, but marketplaces may find it cheaper and easier to store files on a trusted centralized storage platform, instead of running IPFS nodes.

Content storage is particularly an issue with respect to unlockable content. As mentioned earlier, on OpenSea, for example, you can only include text as unlockable content, not image or video files. So, if an NFT minted on OpenSea has an image or video as unlockable content, then the creator has to provide a link to the image or video, which is hosted somewhere on the Internet. It's not likely that your average typical digital artist will be using AWS or another trusted cloud storage provider or the IPFS. More likely, the image or video will be on some website or maybe on Dropbox (a more personal cloud storage provider). But what happens if the artist no longer maintains the website or continues to host it or no longer continues his or her Dropbox account? The image or video would be gone.

Imposters

Just as scammers like to imitate Telegram admins and others, scammers could also imitate a particular NFT artist or other NFT source. In a marketplace, it's important to make sure that the collection from which you're buying an NFT is validated, which is represented by a blue check mark or something similar. Again, the problem here is that you're relying on a trusted third party. Actually, this isn't necessarily a problem; it just obviates the main advantage of a blockchain as discussed earlier by having to rely on a trusted third party.

Although helpful, the validation mark is not a perfect solution. The validating marketplace could make mistakes or even be fooled into validating an imitator. Plus, how would NFT creators not on marketplaces get validated? The bottom line is, even though NFTs prove authenticity of origin, you still need to make sure that the origin is the person they claim to be.

Additional Reproductions

NFTs are unique, right? Yes, they are, and that's a big driver of an NFT's value. But what's preventing the creator of an NFT from making another NFT with the same exact content: same image (or other content), name, description? Nothing, really. Let's say that you bought an NFT, a 1 of 1, and you're feeling good. The next day you see an identical NFT from the same creator. Now you're not feeling so good. You thought you had a unique item and now you don't, and you wouldn't have paid what you did or maybe you wouldn't have even bought the NFT at all.

Some NFTs, such as Rob Gronkowski's "(1-of-1) GRONK Career Highlight Card," say in the description that "This NFT is limited to just 1 edition and will never be minted again." We trust Gronk and the creators of his NFTs. But what about some random artist whose NFT you like?

Claiming something is unique and then creating another identical item is fraud. Likely, the marketplace would boot an artist who did this. But you still may be stuck with an item that you thought was unique that wasn't.

Delivery of Perks and Physical Items

As discussed earlier, an NFT's description can contain perks, such as Rob Gronkowski's "(1-of-1) GRONK Career Highlight Card" NFT. We trust that Gronk, and the company that created his NFTs, will deliver on the perks.

But what can you do if the NFT creator doesn't deliver on the perk or physical item? You may be able to raise the issue with the marketplace on which the NFT was sold, but unfortunately there's not much they can do, other than ban that NFT creator.

The issue here is that perks and physical items aren't really an aspect of an NFT. Perks are more akin to a "Wait... there's more" marketing tactic to increase the value of the NFT. And although a physical item may be the main driver of the value of the NFT, you'll have to trust the NFT creator to deliver them, which obviates the main advantage of blockchain assets: trustless transactions.

Environmental Effects

As discussed in the "Gas Fees" section, transactions on the Ethereum network, the most popular NFT blockchain, currently utilize proof of work to determine who mines a block. As mentioned, proof of work requires massive amounts of computing power, which requires immense amounts of electricity (see Figure 3.4).

If Bitcoin were a country, energy consumption-wise it would fall between the midsize countries of Ukraine and Argentina.

Estimated Annual Energy Consumption (TWh)

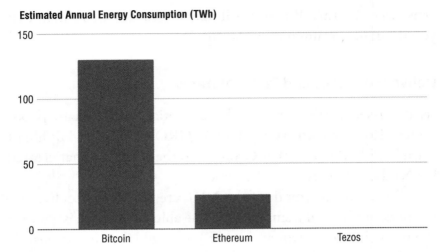

FIGURE 3.4 Estimated annual energy consumption of Bitcoin, Ethereum, and Tezos

Ethereum would be more comparable to Ecuador. Regarding NFTs, (1) Bitcoin has nothing to do with NFTs, and (2) it is estimated that NFTs account for approximately 1 percent of the transactions on the Ethereum network. Personally, 1 percent seems a rather high estimate to us, but let's go with it. This all boils down to an estimated average of 48 kWh per Ethereum transaction, which is less energy than the amount required to make a T-shirt.

Additionally, other NFT blockchains, such as WAX and Tezos, use proof of stake, which consumes 99 percent less energy than proof of work. So, although Bitcoin, Ethereum, and other proof of work blockchains on the whole consume massive amounts of energy, which may have environment effects, NFTs represent a minute portion of this energy consumption. Also, keep in mind that the Ethereum blockchain will be switching to proof of stake in the near future, so virtually all NFTs at that point will be consuming minimal amounts of energy.

Disadvantages of Blockchain

Although decentralized systems, and blockchain in particular, provide several advantages as discussed earlier, they are not perfect either. The following are the main disadvantages of Blockchain.

No Party to Which You Can Appeal. With a decentralized system you're pretty much on your own. If you have an issue, there's no customer support to contact. For example, if you ordered something online with your credit card and the seller never shipped you the item, you could call your credit card company and likely get the charge reversed. Similarly, if you lose your credit card or it gets stolen, you can contact your credit card company and be protected from any fraudulent charges.

> If you purchase something online with cryptocurrency and the seller doesn't ship you the item you purchased, you're out of luck. All cryptocurrency transfers are final and absolute. Once you send cryptocurrency, including an NFT, there's no way to get it back, unless the person to whom you sent it sends it back to you.
>
> This is why it's of utmost importance only to do business with reputable parties when paying with cryptocurrency and buying NFTs. There are a lot of scammers in the crypto space, so you must be extra cautious about those to whom you send cryptocurrency and NFTs.

NFT marketplaces operate as centralized intermediaries between NFT sellers and buyers, and if an issue arises, you can reach out to them for support. However, depending on the issue, there may be little (or nothing) that they can do to help.

Personal Responsibility.   One of the trade-offs of utilizing a system with no intermediaries is personal responsibility. You are responsible for the actions that you take on the blockchain and the resulting consequences. First, as discussed, it's your responsibility to determine the trustworthiness of parties with whom you do business on the blockchain—do your own research (DYOR). Search for reviews, and ask questions in their telegram or other social media channels. You're best off sticking to doing business with known, reputable companies or people. Be extremely wary of scams. If it sounds too good to be true, it probably is.

It's incumbent upon you to keep your cryptocurrency and NFTs safe. If someone gains access to your online banking credentials and transfers money out of your account, you may be able to get that transaction reversed if you contact your bank promptly, usually within 24 hours. If someone gains access to your cryptocurrency wallet and transfers out your crypto and NFTs, you are completely out of luck. It's your responsibility, and yours alone, to keep your wallet's private key safe and protected so it's much less likely to get compromised. We discuss ways to do this in Chapter 6.

Additionally, as mentioned, there are lots of scammers in the cryptocurrency world. Not only will scammers try to get you to send them cryptocurrency, but there are also ones who will ask for your private key.

Never give the private key of your wallet to anyone. Period.

There are a multitude of different kinds of cryptocurrency scams, but here are a few common ones for which you should be on the lookout:

Imposter Websites Scammers go to great lengths to make imposter websites look identical to the original. First, make sure that the site is secure (the address starts with `https`, and the lock icon appears in the address bar). Second, make sure that the domain name is exactly as it should be; no misspellings or a "0" instead of an "O." Also, be careful when typing web addresses into a browser.

Imposter Admins   Telegram and Discord are popular social media platforms, among others, that cryptocurrencies and NFT marketplaces use to build communities and provide updates. Some cryptocurrencies and NFT marketplaces use these platforms for customer service as well, where you can ask questions. Scammers love to pose as fake admins, with the same profile pic as a particular admin, but usually with a slightly different spelling of the username or with an extra letter or period at the end. Make sure that you are conversing with a real admin, who most likely would never ask you to send crypto or an NFT anywhere or ask for your wallet's private key.

Fake Mobile Apps   In addition to fake websites, scammers have been creating fake mobile apps on the Apple App Store and the Google Play Store for years, and people are still falling prey. In February 2021, for example, a person downloaded a fake Trezor app from the App Store and lost nearly all of his life savings: 17.1 Bitcoins, within a second. Apple and Google are trying to crack down, but these scammers are clever. So, make absolutely sure you're downloading the company's (or exchange's or NFT marketplace's, and so on) official app, or you may lose your crypto and/or NFTs.

Scam Emails   Scam and phishing emails can look identical to official emails. Even the "From:" can look like a legit email address. It's imperative that you verify the authenticity of these emails. Call up someone at the company if possible or ask an admin on the company's pertinent social media channel. And never ever click a link in any crypto or NFT-related email unless you are 100 percent certain of its authenticity.

These scams and tips don't just apply to crypto. It's just that in the crypto space, if you make a mistake, it can be devastating, and there's no way to undo it.

Potential Hacks. Like any other system, blockchains and blockchain-related projects are subject to hacks. According to SlowMist Hacked, more than $14.5 billion in value has been lost to blockchain-related hacks. In 2020, hacks occurred in three main areas:

- Decentralized applications (dApps) on the Ethereum network had 47 attacks ($437 million in losses).
- Cryptocurrency exchanges had 28 attacks ($300 million in losses).
- Blockchain wallets had numerous attacks ($3 billion in losses).

Note that these amounts are based on January 2021 cryptocurrency prices.

Your blockchain wallet, where you hold your NFTs, and even an account at a marketplace, can be hacked. In March 2021, some accounts at Nifty Gateway were hacked and thousands of dollars' worth of NFTs were stolen. Apparently, the hack was limited to certain accounts, all of which didn't have two-factor authentication configured. Luckily, this particular hack wasn't more widespread.

Your blockchain wallet is also vulnerable to being hacked if you're not careful. In Chapters 6 and 7, we'll show you how to protect your accounts and blockchain wallet. This is imperative, because if you get hacked, there's nothing that you can do to get your NFTs back.

Keep in mind that tokens can be hacked directly as well. In March 2021, for example, the Paid (PAID) token smart contract was compromised, and a hacker was able to mint himself or herself nearly 60 million tokens, a significant amount of which he or she dumped on the market for a haul of $3 million (see Figure 3.5).

Luckily, the Paid team did the right thing and attempted to make as many investors as whole as possible, and the token seems to have recovered. Other projects weren't so lucky.

Potential Attacks. Blockchains are subject to potential *51 percent attacks*. This is where a group of miners (validators) controls more than 50 percent of the mining power. In such a case, this controlling group could potentially halt transactions between some or all users or, more importantly, reverse recent transactions, allowing them to double-spend coins. In 2018, Bitcoin Gold (BTG) was hit with a 51 percent attack that resulted in double-spending of coins to the tune of $18 million worth.

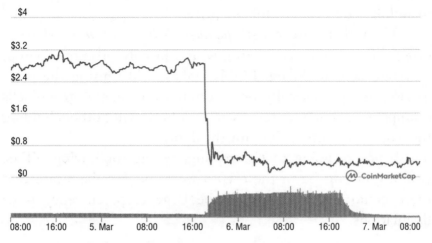

FIGURE 3.5   Paid price chart on the day it was hacked

Abandonment. There are a slew of blockchains that have been abandoned by their founders, otherwise known as *dead coins*. Projects become abandoned due to lack of funding, lack of trading volume, lack of sufficient miners or validators to process transactions, being a scam in the first place, or any combination of the preceding.

Price Volatility. The prices of cryptocurrencies are based purely on market forces, which can lead to significant price volatility. There's no Federal Reserve or other overseeing body setting interest rates or other policies to stabilize values. There's often a crowd mindset with cryptocurrencies, so when a particular coin or token begins to rise, perhaps based on some positive news, fear of missing out (FOMO) may kick in, and the price rockets. At other times, if the price of a coin or token declines, perhaps based on some negative news, panic selling may kick in, and you could get *rekt* (blockchain-speak for "wrecked"). Additionally, for coins and tokens with lower trading volume, it doesn't take many trades to move the price greatly in either direction. Also, there are many *crypto whales* (people who own extremely large amounts of a particular coin or token) who have the potential to manipulate that coin or token's price.

Then there are classic *pump-and-dump schemes*, where a group of people conspire to buy and heavily promote (pump) a certain coin or token. FOMO takes hold causing the price to rise, and at a usually predetermined price, the group sells (dumps) their coins or tokens at a profit, leaving others holding the bag as everyone rushes for the door.

If you're going to be creating, selling, or buying NFTs, you're going to be in the crypto world, so just be aware that there could (most likely will) be large cryptocurrency price fluctuations.

Now that we've covered all the technical reasons why digital assets and NFTs have value, let's explore the external forces that drive the value of NFTs.

External Forces That Drive Value

Let's begin with a question: "Why did Logan Paul's NFTs sell for $5 million?" This story begins with a YouTuber and an uncharacteristic video that spiraled into one of the biggest NFT sales.

Logan Paul, known by most for his high-octane YouTube videos, known by others for his foray into celebrity boxing and his fight against Floyd Mayweather, made a video in October 2020 titled *Opening the $200,000 1st Edition Pokémon Box.*

As with any video on YouTube, clickbait wins. And this clickbait worked! The live-streamed video pulled in more than 300,000 live viewers and more than 11 million total views to date. The event simultaneously raised $130,000 for mental illness.

Clearly, the title piqued people's interest. "What could possibly be contained in a $200,000 Pokémon box, and why would anyone pay that much for some images on cardboard?"

Inside each box were 36 packs of cards with each pack containing 10 Pokémon cards. But it wasn't the collective 360 cards that buyers wanted. It was one card, or rather, one type of card they were seeking: a holographic Pokémon. These are rarer and, therefore, more valuable than their regular counterparts (and look a lot cooler too). If you're lucky enough to pull a holographic Charizard out of a pack, you're looking at a potential value of $350,000. Furthermore, 1st edition boxes were created more than 20 years ago, at the very beginning of the Pokémon card game, which adds to its rarity.

Obviously, the Pokémon franchise doesn't need any help from Logan Paul in order to make sales. Pokémon tops the list of highest-grossing media franchises in the world at approximately $100 billion in total sales, even beating out the likes of Star Wars, Mickey Mouse, and Super Mario.

Although interest in the Pokémon franchise never faded, Logan's video amplified interest in the collectible cards and helped fuel the rage again. His video heavily influenced the resale market of these 1st edition boxes.

Following Logan's video, the resale market for these 1st edition boxes ballooned. Anyone lucky enough to have bought one of these boxes years (or even decades) prior and never opened it was looking at a potential price tag of $300,000–$400,000. For reference, 1st edition boxes were going for around $500 in 2007.

Naturally, Logan wanted to build further on the success of his unboxing video. He did so by creating an even bigger event around his next 1st edition box opening, incorporating a public auction and NFTs.

About four months later, in February 2021, Logan announced another upcoming 1st edition Pokémon box unboxing. But this time, others could get involved in the experience and potentially cash in on the Pokémon collectibles with him.

Logan auctioned off the 36 individual packs within the box. Winning bidders would not only get the contents of the pack, but additionally would be gifted one of Logan's "1st Break" NFTs.

This auction went swimmingly, selling packs for an average of $38,000 for a grand total above $1 million. That's not bad ROI on the $300,000 box.

To add an additional tier for others to get involved, he listed 3,000 editions of his "Box Breaker" NFT at the price of 1 ETH each. Buyers were entered into a lottery, whereby three winners would be chosen at random to be given one of the 36 packs along with a flight to his California studio to attend the live unboxing.

Estimates show that he sold about 2,500 of these additional "lottery ticket" NFTs, and at a price of 1 ETH, he really made out like a bandit. While it's hard to confirm the exact haul he brought in with this entire NFT drop, most estimate it at around $5 million.

The question remains: Were people buying Logan's NFTs because of his status as a creator, and on the basis that his value in society would continue to grow, bringing the value of his NFTs with it? Or, was the price of his "Box Breaker" NFTs justified entirely by another, more popular and existing collectible, the Pokémon cards?

One can make the argument that this wasn't truly an NFT sale, but rather a Pokémon lottery, whereby the tickets were issued and bought in the form of NFTs. And this argument becomes even stronger by the fact that all of Logan's NFTs have plummeted in value since the initial offering. Many of the 1 ETH "Box Breaker" NFTs are being listed and sold at a tenth, or some for even one-hundredth, of the original price.

What can we learn from this?

- Many creators are leaning into physical experiences to enhance the value of their NFTs. As discussed in Chapter 2, most NFT marketplaces allow for unlockable content or perks, such as additional physical goods to be included in the sale of the NFT. Utilizing these features can help parlay something that others already value into NFT value.

- NFT value is volatile. The technology behind NFTs, as discussed in this chapter, prevents frauds and forgeries, as well as supply manipulation. However, the demand of individual NFTs is always subject to change. And as is the case with Logan's NFTs, when the unlockable, physical experience was used up, the price of the digital part of the NFT dropped because the assumed value was encompassed in the physical unlockable.

We tell this story to address the cross-pollination between the traditional collectibles market and digital collectibles. The lines are still quite blurry as to whether NFT values will continue to appreciate. And for many creators jumping into the space, they're leaning heavily on what's worked historically in the physical collectibles space and parlaying it into a digital collectible.

In many cases, there isn't enough demand for a person's NFT because who really knows whether or not that demand will increase over time. Therefore, there's no assurance that the value of the NFT will rise. This is why Logan's pairing with Pokémon was one part genius and one part antithetical to the purpose of NFTs, which are supposed to be digital assets.

While intrinsically the technology behind NFTs is what makes them scarce and, therefore, gives them the ability to have value, there's still no rhyme or reason as to what NFTs or which NFT creators will continue on a trajectory of high demand. As we established, collectible value is largely dependent on the demands of the market. The more people who want something, the higher the price goes.

Ideally, Logan continues to break barriers and grow as a creator (and boxer). Theoretically, his NFT collectible cards should mirror the growth of his brand. But there are still too many unknowns in the NFT market to say for sure whether NFT values will grow in parallel to the people creating and collecting them. The market will decide.

4

History of NFTs

As with the history of anything, it's challenging to point to an exact moment in time and say, "This is what started that." Rather, there are moments that precipitate a change. These small moments run parallel to each other until they converge to create something special.

With regard to non-fungible tokens (NFTs), the history can be quite blurry. It wouldn't be correct to start talking about NFTs at the moment that the first blockchain was built in 2008, because that would ignore the decades of digital art up to that point that provided a reason for NFTs to exist. It also wouldn't be fair to cover only digital art and overlook other art movements that would change the profile of art collectors and thus expand the group of people collecting art.

The story of Andy Warhol and Pop Art, the legend of Mike Winkelmann and his Cyberpunk creations, and of course, the rich history of digital art innovators have all played a crucial role in the history of NFTs.

Andy Warhol Presents Pop Art

Throughout the 1950s, years before the creation of *Campbell's Soup Cans* or the *Marilyn Diptych*, you could find Andy Warhol at a New York City café called Serendipity. Here, he would trade his drawings for pastries and ice cream, while getting to glance at the celebrity elite of New York City.

A stone's throw away from Madison Avenue, Warhol had his sights set on the advertising industry. Having grown up a poor Slovakian immigrant during the Great Depression—a time when his mother might replace a basic can of tomato soup for ketchup and water—Warhol was enthralled by the Post-War capitalist boom. Factories rolled out products allowing access to quality goods for even the least fortunate.

Later, Warhol would say:

> "What's great about this country is America started the tradition where the richest consumers buy essentially the same things as the poorest. You can be watching TV and see Coca-Cola, and you can know that the President drinks Coke, Liz Taylor drinks Coke, and just think, you can drink Coke, too. A Coke is a Coke, and no amount of money can get you a better Coke than the one the bum on the corner is drinking. All the Cokes are the same and all the Cokes are good."

Consumerism was taking shape. And Warhol wanted in.

Warhol found great success on Madison Avenue providing illustrations in magazines and advertisements for clientele such as *Glamour* magazine and Tiffany & Co. His portfolio of commercial art gained him a lot of respect among ad men and consumers, and it even spanned large enough for an entire posthumous exhibition titled *Warhol Before Pop*.

But as his bank account grew, so did his ambitions. He wanted respect in the fine art world—not just as a commercial illustrator.

Despite the name he had made for himself, Warhol didn't explode as an artist to start. His first exhibition at the Ferus Gallery in West Hollywood, California, featured the now iconic 32-piece collection of *Campbell's Soup Cans*. He managed to sell only one piece and receive holds on four other pieces. Call it foresight or call it luck, one of the gallery owners, Irving Blum, decided to cancel the four holds and buy back the fifth work. He then came to an agreement with Warhol to buy the entire lot on layaway at the price of $100 a month for 10 months. (About 26 years later, the Museum of Modern Art purchased the collection for $15 million.)

Following the showcase, Warhol continued honing his craft and leaning into the Pop Art movement that was well underway.

Pop Art was unique in that it was the first aesthetic that invited everyone to participate and appreciate. Pop Art threw its nose up at elitist culture and replaced it with popular culture as its muse. Comic book characters, popular ads, and mass-produced products were the main fixtures in Pop Art.

Pop Art was the first art movement accessible to the average person. And this was something that Warhol knew all too well.

Warhol continued creating art that reflected this emerging society of consumerism. He took images from commercial art and pop culture, focusing on some of the most familiar or banal components of the American environment, and he changed them slightly to showcase them in another light.

Campbell's Soup Cans, *Marilyn Diptych*, *Coca-Cola 3*, *Triple Elvis*, *Brillo Box*, and many others all contributed to this "accessible" art. He magnified his artwork by building a reserved and mysterious celebrity persona. He surrounded himself with artists and celebrities. All of this helped him grow into a living icon, and thus a Pop Art piece himself.

Although Pop Art was largely defined by its ironic approach, you don't get the sense Andy was trying to be ironic with his art. Rather, his aim was to expand the appreciation of art by highlighting the images that we encounter daily but don't actually take the time to look at. Packaging labels, celebrities, photos of disasters—these were his subjects.

Warhol's style succeeded Marcel Duchamp's *readymade*, a style of art created from undisguised, but often modified, everyday objects or products not normally considered materials from which art is made. Similarly, Warhol's Pop Art reminded us of the art around us, giving us no choice but to look at the products of society as art. Whether the subject of his art was a recognizable person, a household product, or an image that everyone saw in the news, Warhol became an art remixer. He took images of what we consumed, duplicated the image, added popping color, and ultimately created something familiar enough that you recognized its subject immediately but also fresh enough where you had to look deeper because there was something else there. By highlighting consumerism, he put us all, as cogs in the machine of capitalism, into the artwork, thus lifting the veil so that we could look closer at our environments.

Decades later, Warhol's aesthetic still provides an easy foray into art appreciation for many newcomers. He stripped away technical detail and depth, replacing it with simplicity—almost as if an homage to his early days in the advertising industry.

Warhol's legacy spans many different innovations:

- He helped change the perception of the artist from the ideator and creator into simply the designer of the art, whether or not the artist actually puts the pen to paper or brush to canvas.

- Many point to him as the earliest visionary of the coming reality TV and personal branding movement.

In our mind, however, the legacy that we owe most to Warhol, and the legacy for which NFTs owe a lot of thanks, is his refreshing and renewed understanding in what can pass as art.

While not the originator of Pop Art, Warhol quickly became the champion, the figurehead of this motif.

Pop Art is responsible for democratizing the appreciation of art. Because the subject matter of Pop Art pieces included some element of popular culture, the average consumer was able to recognize instantly who or what was in the artwork. There was no prior knowledge needed other than being a person who consumed things. By simply buying Brillo soap pads, reading the daily comics, or going to the movies, you were able to appreciate Pop Art.

Without this movement, there wouldn't be nearly as many art collectors at all levels of income as we have today. Our idea of what passes as an artwork that can appreciate in value would not be nearly as expansive. As a result, we can make the connection that there wouldn't be an emerging community for NFTs and digital art collectibles such as NBA Top Shot, Logan Paul Box Breakers, CryptoKitties, and even Beeple's NFTs—all of which could be classified as Pop Art.

Undoubtedly, we owe a debt of gratitude to Warhol for his ideas and his vision. Never confined by the medium, Warhol made art with everything from silkscreens to printmaking to photography, video cameras, and even Xerox machines. But a lesser-known technique of his that doesn't quite get the coverage it deserves was his dabbling in early digital art technology.

The year was 1985. The computing company Commodore was announcing its new Amiga 1000 personal computer at New York City's Lincoln Center. To one-up Apple's paramount Macintosh commercial in 1984, Commodore enlisted Warhol and Debbie Harry to show off the computer's ProPaint feature in action.

About three-quarters of the way through the event, Andy sat down at an Amiga, snapped a digital photo of Debbie, uploaded it into the Amiga, and began digitally altering the portrait of Debbie in a style similar to the *Marilyn Diptych*. After a minute or so, the digital portrait was done.

Resident Amiga artist, Jack Hager, then asked Warhol, "What computers have you worked on before?" To which Warhol replied, "Oh, I haven't worked on anything. I've waited for this one."

Unbeknownst to the viewer, it appeared to be a typical celebrity endorsement. But it wasn't. Not only was Warhol enlisted to market this new technology, he actually used it in his free time.

Warhol created a short film with the Amiga 1000 entitled *You Are The One*. The film featured 20 digitized images of Marilyn Monroe from 1950s newsreel footage, which Warhol manipulated with the Amiga and set to music.

After his death, Warhol's Amiga computer and floppy discs were stored in the archives of the Warhol Museum. Forgotten, but not gone. Nearly three decades later, the Carnegie Museum of Art was sparked by inspiration to actually recover Warhol's digital artwork. With some careful reverse-engineering, the team unearthed somewhere around 20 never-before-seen digital artworks by Warhol.

Although, unfortunately, Warhol wasn't around long enough to see digital art take center stage in the art world, his contribution is but one small story in the canon of digital art.

Had Warhol been born a lifetime later, we could certainly see him taking a similar path in digital art that Mike Winkelmann, also known as Beeple or Beeple_Crap, has done for the past decade and a half.

Beeple's Cyberpunk World Meets NFTs

It's rare for an artist to receive their flowers before they've passed away. It's even rarer for a prototypical, unassuming computer science nerd with a potty mouth to become the face of an entire art movement known as *digital art*, let alone sell an art piece for more than $69 million at a high-society Christie's auction.

"What can one person and a computer do? That has always been a really cool concept to me, because it's the equalizer, in a way," Mike Winkelmann said in an interview with *The New Yorker*.

Born to humble, Midwestern roots in Wisconsin, Winkelmann was on the computer science track from an early age. He attended Purdue University with the goal of learning to program video games, but quickly found himself working on his own endeavors in lieu of school. He slogged through the degree, was released into the world with computer skills, and got a job as a web designer.

His fascination with computers and art collided in his free time. One of his first areas of success in the motion graphics space was creating video loops for DJ sets. Think of abstract shapes and lights that you find at an EDM concert today. As an aspiring DJ, he designed them for himself but eventually allowed others to download and experiment with them for free.

Just a man and his computer, Winkelmann was mesmerized by the virtual worlds and digital creations that one could create on the computer with modeling and visual effects software such as Cinema 4D. He had the technical prowess to dive headfirst into these tools, but he lacked the artistic ability. He needed to learn how to draw.

Around 2007, Winkelmann got the idea, from a sketch artist named Tom Judd, of creating something every single day: the concept of getting better incrementally by going from zero to completion in a day was exactly what he wanted.

And so, Beeple's *Everydays* were born.

The first year of *Everydays* mostly consisted of sketches, self-portraits, and doodles. Then the Beeple_Crap we know today started taking shape. He began learning Cinema 4D before the eyes of his audience, improving day over day.

Cyberpunk became the main motif of his *Everydays*—building utopian and dystopian still images with the best motion graphic software on the market.

The Cyberpunk aesthetic has a thriving community of supporters with roots dating back to the 1960s. As a clear-cut antithesis to many of the utopian dreams early technology proponents envisioned, Cyberpunk looked at dystopian futuristic settings—often juxtaposing high technological achievements with a radical breakdown of social order.

Rooted in the unstoppable progress of technology, Cyberpunk was made for the society we live in today, and it will only continue to feel closer to reality as we progress. Furthermore, Cyberpunk has benefitted from its many decades of artistry and has therefore, built a great audience for its themes.

From the early beginnings of Philip K. Dick and Isaac Asimov novels to Ridley Scott's *Blade Runner*, the paramount manga film *Akira, The Matrix Trilogy, Minority Report*, Netflix's *Black Mirror* series, and thousands of more works, our society cannot get enough Cyberpunk. It's as if we prefer consuming the dystopian nightmares that seem so close to our reality, as opposed to utopian visions.

History of NFTs **101**

Beeple couldn't have chosen a better aesthetic around which to build his *Everydays*.

No matter the circumstances, Winkelmann continued creating a piece every day from scratch. No pre-planning or pre-creating his *Everydays*. No archive of work that he could lean on when he felt lazy. Just a man and his computer. Chris Do of the media brand The Futur likened Winkelmann's process to that of Michael Shattuck—the man who runs 365 marathons a year.

Winkelmann, 5000+ *Everydays* later, has created one of the most prolific archives of digital artwork known to man. And he's built an incredible audience of Cyberpunk lovers in the process of sharing *Everydays*. Never one to brag or boast about his work (as is customary for Wisconsin-bred residents), Beeple still claims to "suck ass" at motion design. But glancing through his archive of work, you can see the growth of an artist.

Winkelmann's *Everydays* made him popular as a designer for commercial work—SpaceX, Apple, Nike, Louis Vuitton, Super Bowls, concerts—you name it. Beeple has created a career for himself, simply by doing what he loved.

Before NFTs, this was the livelihood of a digital artist: make incredible work to get recognized by the corporate world for campaigns.

In the past few years or so, Beeple's *Everydays* started getting weirder than ever, for lack of a better term (see Figure 4.1). His works included Donald Trump lactating, Mickey Mouse being sucked of his innards, and a giant naked Elon Musk riding a giant Shiba Inu, the dog of the Dogecoin logo. He didn't stray from the Cyberpunk aesthetic; however, he mixed it with pop culture characters to create a sort of nightmare reality for viewers.

FIGURE 4.1 Three works by Beeple: *Birth of a Nation*, *Disneyworld 2020*, and *Non-Fungible Elon*

In an interview with Kara Swisher of *The New York Times'* Sway podcast, Beeple describes his art:

> "The thing I'm trying to reflect is there are some very weird things happening with technology. Some very unintended consequences. And I believe that is only going to accelerate. I think Donald Trump was a very weird unintended consequence of technology that we did not see."

The Cyberpunk subtleties that commanded his work were now transposed over the world we all inhabited. In much the same way that Warhol's Pop Art examined consumerism as it was being established, Beeple's Cyberpunk art examines technocentrism as it's taking shape in all facets of life.

Beeple was not ahead of the curve on cryptocurrency, blockchain, or NFTs. He was right on time.

In October 2020, Beeple released his first NFT, which sold for $66,666.66 (and was resold for 100x at $6.6 million a few months later). In December 2020, he followed this up with a series of works that were sold for $3.5 million. Then just a few months later, working with MakersPlace (an NFT marketplace), the Christie's auction house approached Mike to do an NFT drop. Christie's convinced him to package the first 5,000 *Everydays* into an NFT, which then sold for more than $69 million.

In our minds, Beeple's *Everydays* were the perfect collection for a transaction of this magnitude. Why? The fact that Beeple is a digital-native artist who leaned into technology to create art, then focused his art on examining technology, and finally benefitted from a groundbreaking technology to sell his work . . . is the perfect story. Would it have been as eye-opening if the largest NFT transaction was from an established artist like Jeff Koons? Certainly not.

Cyberpunk is likely the perfect motif to usher in the era of NFTs, given that it's a style of art that directly examines many of the technologies used to create, market, and sell NFTs. The aesthetic is more relevant than ever, given that nearly all of our behaviors are influenced by algorithms, and not a minute goes by where we aren't aided by (or addicted to) technology.

Beeple's foresight to stick with Cyberpunk was ideal. He ultimately benefited from staying motivated for more than 13 years and creating an immense archive of work.

Whether he likes it or not, Beeple is now the poster child for NFTs, in the same way that Warhol was the poster child for Pop Art. Ideally, his continued work will raise the tide for digital-native artists everywhere, who much like Winkelmann, have relied on client work or printing their digital art into physical media to make money.

While Beeple has the largest digital art transaction to date, it's unfair to gloss over the rich history of digital art and all of the disrespect artists in this medium had to endure for decades, being told that their medium wasn't "real art." The story of digital art goes way back, long before Winkelmann decided to make his first *Everyday*.

The Story of Digital Art

What is art? A quick Google search will populate a million different answers, actually 13 billion to be exact. The simple fact is that not a single one of those 13 billion answers does the scope of art justice because every time it is defined, we pigeonhole art and leave something out. It's as if by defining art, we leave the door open for an individual to come through and expose us to a form of art that we hadn't thought of.

For centuries, art meant paintings, frescoes, sculptures, music, and poetry. A looser definition might have included immaculate buildings like the Parthenon or the Pyramids at Giza.

Then, Marcel Duchamp flipped the world on its head and said that an artist is someone who can point a finger and say "that's art." And he demonstrated this by putting a toilet in a gallery. Later, Warhol flipped it again by pointing the finger at ourselves, more or less claiming that our collective human behavior is a form of art. He elaborated on this by saying that art is what you can get away with. And just when we thought we encompassed everything, food became art. Michelin star restaurants began showing how food could be a medium for creative expression.

Artists throughout time have done their best to break barriers and bring society into uncomfortable spaces—places we hadn't recognized as art before. Even though entire cultures sprang up out of graffiti, namely, hip-hop culture and skate culture, graffiti wasn't respected holistically until Art Basel hired graffiti artists to tag the entire city of Miami.

The story of art is the story of breaking barriers. One visionary does something different and calls it art. The art world either respects it, copies it, or pushes it aside. But eventually, all forms of artistic expression, no matter how outlandish, find a following.

For digital art, it didn't take long to find its community of supporters. But to this day, it still struggles to convince many of its value to society. Nonetheless, the story of digital art is a prehistory to NFTs. Because without digital artists, there's largely no reason for NFTs to exist.

Digital Art Emerges

In the early 1950s at an army surplus warehouse in Manchester, England, a man by the name of Desmond Paul Henry stumbled upon a mint-condition Sperry bombsight computer. One of the many computers developed during WWII, the Sperry was fixed onto bomber aircraft and used to determine the exact moment to release a bomb in order to hit the target. By the 1950s, it was an outdated technology in war, but a fresh tool for the art world. At least, that's what Henry believed.

Henry would tinker with the Sperry throughout the 1950s, marveling at its construction. Ultimately, though, he wanted to find some way to visualize its abilities. So, he fastened a plotter (basically a pen at the end of an arm) onto the machine and began tweaking the mechanics to see what it could draw.

Unlike the algorithmically generated art that followed throughout the 1960s and 1970s, Henry's drawing machine relied entirely on the "mechanics of chance," in other words, the relationship between the plotter and the machine's mechanical components. For example, a loosened screw could dramatically change the final result.

Because his computer could not be preprogrammed nor store information, each drawing was entirely random. He could tweak the machine's mechanical components, but he had no clue how it would affect the drawing. This imprecise construction meant that Henry's creations could never be replicated or mass-produced. Each one was entirely unique. The first artwork

FIGURE 4.2   First artwork from the Henry Drawing Machine

the Henry Drawing Machine came back with is pictured in Figure 4.2.

Doesn't it look like an abstract painting that you might find in a gallery somewhere, with dozens of connoisseurs surrounding it, analyzing the meaning behind the artist's vision?

Unfortunately, this wasn't the case. *Computer art*, as it was referred to back in those times, was not particularly respected by the art world. Perhaps this was because computers were lifeless machines that crunched numbers all day, or they resembled the machines that churned out Coca-Colas on a factory line. Or, perhaps it was because their creators were nerds who obsessed over the minutiae of something no one understood, not eccentric and lively artists with whom you'd love to have a conversation.

Regardless of the reasons, computer art remained the distant step-cousin of the art world for decades. "It's not *real* art" was the popular and entirely ridiculous response to this style of creation.

Despite the hate, believers in computer art chugged along and formed their own communities of support.

In 1967, the nonprofit Experiments in Art and Technology was formed following a series of performances the previous year called "9 Evenings: Theatre and Engineering," where 10 contemporary artists joined forces with 30 engineers and scientists from Bell Labs to showcase the use of new technologies in art.

In 1968, the Institute of Contemporary Arts in London hosted one of the most influential early exhibitions of computer art, called "Cybernetic Serendipity." Also in 1968, the Computer Arts Society was founded to promote the use of computers in artwork.

Throughout the 1960s and 1970s, much of the digital art created was dependent on the use of mathematics, using early algorithms and math to generate abstract art. Digital art was almost entirely siloed to the engineers interested in pushing the limits of technology or the few artists who had the foresight to test this new form of creation.

Artistry has always required a technical understanding of the medium used, along with an understanding of art composition. Whether the medium is pastel on canvas, graphite on paper, or chisel against marble, the technical understanding of how the materials react with the surface wasn't insurmountable. It just took practice.

Early digital art was no different in that you had to understand the medium, which at the time meant understanding how computers operated. For this reason, many of the early digital artists were computer programmers.

Then a tectonic shift happened in 1984 that would change not only "how" computer art was created but more importantly "who" could create it.

Steve Jobs was on the scene at Apple, and his first major release was the Macintosh computer, whose main advantage was the *graphical user interface (GUI)*. GUIs were paramount in that they presented computing through icons and windows, allowing the average person to interact with computers. Not to mention, for just $195, Mac users could purchase MacPaint and have the ability to create their own digital art. Personal computers gave every artist the ability to create digital art. As we discussed earlier in this chapter, Commodore followed up Apple the following year with its Amiga 1000 computer and the Deluxe Paint software.

In the decade that followed, iconic software developed specifically for the purposes of creating digital art began popping up: Adobe Photoshop in 1988 and Corel Painter in 1990, for example. And then in 1992, Wacom created one of the first tablet computers where users interacted with the computer through a cordless stylus—a digital artist's dream.

Because software made the creation of digital art easier, more artists began using the tools and forming communities to share their experiences. Recognizing that digital art was taking off but had no central place to display, the Austin Museum of Digital Art was launched in 1997, entirely for the display and promotion of digital creations. A couple of years later, the Digital Art Museum launched the first online museum for digital art. (And a little over a decade later, the Museum of Modern Art came to its senses and created a Digital Art Vault containing more than 4,000 works of digital art.)

Coupling these emerging digital art communities with the increasing use of visual effects in movies and complex virtual worlds in video games meant that more of society was being exposed to digital art throughout the 1980s and 1990s, whether they recognized it or not.

When Henry was building his Henry Drawing Machine in the 1950s, he wasn't concerned with the art world not respecting his creations. He believed it to be art. Early digital artists were breaking barriers and taking the brunt of the hate for it. Just a few decades later, digital art was taking over the world. And people were finally beginning to appreciate it.

Digital Art Starts to Sell

Unsurprisingly, the Internet lent a major hand to the growth of digital art. Launched in 2005, `Behance.net` became the de facto place to share one's portfolio of digital art and land commercial projects. Emi Haze, for example, built a strong following on Behance and landed projects with Apple and Wacom and even became one of the few digital artists honored during Adobe's 25th Anniversary.

Flash-forward to 2013 when one of the most monumental moments in digital art history took place. The Phillips Auction House and Tumblr teamed up to hold the first-ever digital art auction, selling 16 pieces of digital art for a total of $90,600. Although various blockchains existed at the time, they didn't employ the technology to secure the rights of this digital artwork. Rather, they simply delivered to each buyer a hard drive containing a file of the work.

Just a year later, though, blockchain and art would finally collide for the first-ever NFT, or, as they referred to it at the time, *monetized graphics*.

In 2014, an event called Seven on Seven was held in New York City. Designed much like a hackathon, where artists and technologists are brought together to collaborate and spark ideas, one of the random pairings occurred between Kevin McCoy and Anil Dash. Dash was working as a consultant to auction houses; McCoy, as a digital artist and professor at New York University.

This was during Tumblr's heyday, when digital assets of all kinds were shared far and wide, often without any attribution at all. McCoy was one of the many digital artists whose works went viral on Tumblr, but he didn't receive very much credit, or any remuneration. Needless to say, he was already looking into the application of blockchain to digital art.

In an article in *The Atlantic*, Dash outlined the event:

"By the wee hours of the night, McCoy and I had hacked together a first version of a blockchain-backed means of asserting ownership over an original digital work. Exhausted and a little loopy, we gave our creation an ironic name: monetized graphics. Our first live demonstration was at the New Museum of Contemporary Art in New York City, where the mere phrase *monetized graphics* prompted knowing laughter from an audience wary of corporate-sounding intrusions into the creative arts. McCoy used a blockchain called Namecoin to register a video clip that his wife had previously made, and I bought it with the four bucks in my wallet... But the NFT prototype we created in a one-night hackathon had some shortcomings. You couldn't store the actual digital artwork in a blockchain; because of technical limits, records in most blockchains are too small to hold an entire image... Seven years later, all of today's popular NFT platforms still use the same shortcut."

Although McCoy and Dash didn't pursue the idea further, they demonstrated the possibilities. And that was enough for the time being.

Just a year later, QuHarrison Terry and Ryan Cowdrey co-founded 23VIVI, the world's first digital art marketplace using the Bitcoin blockchain to create certificates of authenticity.

Cowdrey recalls:

"Selling digital art in 2015 was no laughing matter. First of all, we were using the Bitcoin blockchain to create proof of ownership. This was super slow. Especially when compared to the Ethereum blockchain that is used for most NFTs today. But the other main roadblock was the market. People didn't understand digital art, let alone consider purchasing it. So, we leaned on our connections. More than half of all our sales started with our friends and family. And even then, it was a challenge convincing a friend to spend $20 on a digital file."

Find any early digital art dealer, and they'll tell you a similar story about selling their first pieces to friends and family.

In an interview with Gary Vaynerchuk, the cofounder of CryptoKitties, Mik Naayem said the following:

"When we created CryptoKitties, I was trying to get all of my friends to buy CryptoKitties. And I couldn't. Like they'd look at me, they'd look at the cats and be like 'this is complicated.'"

Little did they know that CryptoKitties would catch on and become one of the first instances of NFT success. So, what are CryptoKitties?

The Internet has a unique relationship with cats to say the least. The Internet has famous cats such as Grumpy Cat, Lil Bub, Nyan Cat, and Colonel Meow. In 2015, CNN estimated that there were more than 6.5 billion pictures of cats on the Internet. One of the earliest reasons for people to go on YouTube was to watch funny cat videos, and it's estimated that today YouTube videos featuring felines as the main subject have racked up more than 26 billion views. ThoughtCatalog has even coined them the official mascot of the Internet.

Therefore, it should come as no surprise that the first NFTs to reach a critical mass were a collection of NFTs featuring digital cat artworks. Launched in November 2017 by Dapper Labs, CryptoKitties are an Ethereum blockchain game where users can buy, collect, breed, and sell virtual cats. The game was launched with 100 "Founder Kitties," with one "Gen 0" cat released every 15 minutes. The game was a nearly instant hit.

TechCrunch reported a few days after the launch that more than $1.3 million had already been transacted for CryptoKitties.

FIGURE 4.3 Three CryptoKitties: #1, Genesis; #222, Koshkat; and #1992771, Holly

The blockchain game had such a demand that it accounted for more than 15 percent of Ethereum's network traffic at the end of 2017. Three CryptoKitties are pictured in Figure 4.3.

These were more than a Beanie Baby–like collectible, though. The game offered a unique breeding (or as they refer to it, *siring*) feature. Basically, an owner puts their CryptoKitty up to sire for a specified amount of Ethereum (ETH). When someone agrees to that price, the two CryptoKitties breed. The person who put their kitty up for sire gets the Ethereum, and the other owner receives the resulting CryptoKitty.

Coded into each kitten is a 256-bit genome that holds the genetic sequence to all of the different combinations that kittens can have. Background color, cooldown time, whiskers, beards, stripes, and so on are all of the "genes" that these CryptoKitties can have.

The demand for certain "cattributes" grew in the community of collectors. Dapper Labs never set a rarity on the different features. What collectors wanted grew entirely organically.

Less than four months later, with an Internet commerce phenomenon on their hands, the team behind CryptoKitties raised $12 million from acclaimed investors such as Union Square Ventures and Andreessen Horowitz. Since then, Dapper Labs has rolled out NBA Top Shots, has its own blockchain called Flow, and has UFC-themed digital collectibles in the works.

Undoubtedly, CryptoKitties has played a massive role in raising the awareness of owning digital assets. Who knows where we'd be today without them?

We cannot talk about digital art hits without mentioning Curio Cards or CryptoPunks, the first and second (respectively) NFT projects to store proof of ownership on the Ethereum blockchain.

Curio Cards, launched on May 9, 2017, feature 30 unique series of NFT cards from 7 different artists. The project was largely created to show a new model for digital art ownership, in many ways, as an example for others to follow. To show its age, Curio Cards were developed before the ERC-721 NFT standard was proposed (the standard used on marketplaces like OpenSea today)—making them somewhat obsolete. However, they developed a token contract that allows owners to "wrap" their Curio Card in another token, thus making them functional on modern NFT marketplaces.

Artistically, Curio Cards took this revolutionary technology to heart and designed the series of cards to tell the story of mankind up to digital art. Starting with #1, featuring an apple that represents the creation story, and ending with #30, featuring the first GIF ever created.

And then there were CryptoPunks. Launched in June 2017 by Larva Labs, CryptoPunks are 10,000 unique collectible characters created in the style of Pixel Art, which has a rich history dating back to games like *Space Invaders* and *Pac-Man*. When they launched, Larva Labs literally gave CryptoPunks away to anyone who'd accept them. In 2021, OpenSea estimates the total volume of CryptoPunks transacted at more than 172,000 ETH, with nine CryptoPunks being sold for a collective $17 million in May 2021.

While many digital artists and collectors have found success over the past few years in NFTs and the headline-grabbing transaction sizes seem to be getting bigger and more absurd, they wouldn't be here without the rich history of digital artists before them.

The pioneers who experimented with technology to create digital art, the early adopters who started events and galleries to promote digital art, and the first innovators in blockchain-backed digital art who pushed digital art ownership into the foreground laid the foundation for the Beeples, the Gronkowskis, and the CryptoKitties to thrive.

In the words of Isaac Newton, "If I have seen further, it is by standing on the shoulders of giants." The giants in the world of digital art had to put up with droves of people saying that their art wasn't "real art." And while they may never receive the credit (nor the dollars) that they deserve, they made it possible for digital artists of all kinds to monetize their creations in the medium for which they intended it.

CHAPTER

5

NFT Marketplaces

If you're looking to create, sell, or buy non-fungible tokens (NFTs), your best bet would be to do it on one of the many NFT marketplaces. By creating and minting an NFT on a marketplace, you won't need to know how to code a smart contract or need any technical knowledge at all. This is a major breakthrough that allows the average person to create and mint NFTs.

Of course, you're still going to need to get on the blockchain because NFTs are blockchain assets. We'll guide you through this, as well as with the creating, minting, selling, and buying of NFTs in Chapters 6–8. We'll be using OpenSea, the largest and most popular marketplace, as the platform on which we will guide you. Nonetheless, we recommend that you explore all of the marketplaces detailed in this chapter. Each has its own character, focus, and community. By exploring them all, you will get a broader sense of the overall NFT market.

This chapter provides an overview of several of the most popular NFT marketplaces.

OpenSea

Website: `Opensea.io`

OpenSea is the largest and most popular NFT marketplace. It also claims to be the first as well. As of this writing, OpenSea features 15.5 million NFTs and has sold $354 million of NFTs.

We find OpenSea to be the easiest to navigate and most user-friendly when creating, selling, and buying NFTs. It's great for beginners who are just getting into NFTs. Collectors can also find a wide variety of NFTs on OpenSea, including the following:

- Digital art
- Collectibles
- Music
- Domain names
- Virtual real estate
- Digital trading cards
- In-game items

You can choose various ways to sell your NFTs, including English auctions and Dutch auctions.

Overall, we highly recommend OpenSea, which is why we use it as the go-to marketplace in the chapters that follow.

Pros
- Largest NFT marketplace
- Easy to create, sell, and buy NFTs
- Free to mint NFTs

- Only a one-time double gas fee to list NFTs for sale
- Fee of only 2.5 percent of sales

Cons
- Can buy and sell NFTs only with cryptocurrency
- Based on the Ethereum blockchain, which can have high gas prices for transactions

Rarible

Website: Rarible.com

Like OpenSea, *Rarible* is user-friendly and easy to navigate, and you can create, sell, and buy various types of NFTs.

Rarible has incorporated some social media elements into its site, such as a "follow" feature, allowing users to follow NFT creators and get notified when the creator drops new NFTs.

Rarible also created the RARI token, which is the native governance token of the NFT marketplace, designed to reward active platform users with a voice on the platform's future.

Rarible takes a 5 percent commission from every sale, charging 2.5 percent to both the buyer and the seller.

Pros
- Easy to create, sell, and buy NFTs
- Vibrant community

Cons
- Can buy and sell NFTs only with cryptocurrency
- Based on the Ethereum blockchain, which can have high gas prices for transactions
- Must pay a gas fee every time you mint an NFT

Nifty Gateway

Website: `Niftygateway.com`

NFTs are called *nifties* on *Nifty Gateway*. The marketplace sells nifties of only established digital artists, celebrities, and brands. For example, Nifty Gateway featured drops by Beeple, Deadmau5, Eminem, and Paris Hilton.

Nifty Gateway portrays itself as a high-end marketplace, like an exclusive art gallery. Creators need to apply and go through an extensive vetting process to sell on Nifty Gateway.

Nifty Gateway is one of the rare marketplaces where you can purchase NFTs with a credit or debit card, which opens up nifties to collectors not familiar with cryptocurrency.

Pros
- Can buy nifties with a credit or debit card
- Easy and intuitive to use

Cons
- Fee of 15 percent of sales
- Sellers need to create a Gemini account to cash out
- Need to apply to sell nifties
- Based on the Ethereum blockchain, which can have high gas prices for transactions

SuperRare

Website: `Superrare.co`

As the name implies, *SuperRare* sells only single-edition (1 of 1) NFTs. Additionally, only digital art NFTs are sold on SuperRare, which are not available for purchase anywhere else.

SuperRare describes itself as "Instagram meets Christie's. A new way to interact with art, culture, and collecting on the Internet!"

SuperRare has built a strong community, and it also tracks the top collectors and trending artists.

Like Nifty Gateway, SuperRare has an elegant design. Additionally, an editorial section of the website features a few digital art-related articles each day, akin to a glossy art magazine.

Pros
- Rare, single-edition NFTs
- Easy and intuitive to use
- Strong community

Cons
- Fee of 15 percent of primary sales
- Need to apply to sell NFTs
- Based on the Ethereum blockchain, which can have high gas prices for transactions

Wax (Atomic Hub)

Website: Wax.atomichub.io

Atomic Hub is based on the *WAX blockchain*, which is entirely separate from the Ethereum (ETH) blockchain. WAX is not as popular as ETH, but WAX transaction fees are minimal compared to ETH gas fees. Additionally, WAX uses proof-of-stake validation, which means that it has negligible effects on the environment.

Atomic Hub is most notable for selling packs of NFTs, like a pack of baseball cards, where you don't know what you're going to get inside the pack. Similarly, NFTs found in packs have different levels of rareness. For example, Topps sells packs of Major League Baseball NFTs, which are traded on an active secondary market.

Pros
- No ETH gas fees
- Environmentally friendly
- Only 2 percent fee on sales of NFTs

Cons
- Creating NFTs is complicated.
- The WAX blockchain is much less popular than the ETH blockchain.
- NFTs are not transferable to the ETH blockchain.

Foundation

Website: `Foundation.app`

Foundation calls itself a "playground" for artists, curators, and collectors. The marketplace design seems heavily influenced by social media, particularly Instagram. Users are encouraged to link their social media to their Foundation account.

Anyone can sign up, but if you want to sell your NFTs, you have to be upvoted by other community members. This community-led curation makes it more difficult to sell your NFTs but maintains a certain level of quality of the artwork.

Pros
- Nice variety of quality art NFTs
- Active community of artists and collectors

Cons

- Fee of 15 percent of primary sales
- No way to filter searches
- Based on the Ethereum blockchain, which can have high gas prices for transactions

NBA Top Shot

Website: NBAtopshot.com

Created by Dapper Labs, the creator of CryptoKitties, *NBA Top Shot* is a marketplace where you can buy video NFTs of historical NBA moments. The marketplace has been wildly popular, with hundreds of millions of dollars in sales.

Like Atomic Hub, collectors buy packs of unknown NFTs of varying rarity, which they can then sell on the secondary market.

Collectors can also compete in challenges to earn free NFTs.

The marketplace is on the FLOW blockchain, which uses proof-of-stake validation, like WAX.

Pros

- Awesome NBA video NFTs
- Environmentally friendly
- Can purchase NFTs with your credit or debit card

Cons

- NFTs are not transferable to the ETH blockchain.
- It can take weeks to withdraw funds.
- Market gets flooded with NFTs due to the regular release of new packs.

VeVe

Website: `Veve.me`

Veve is a mobile app, available on the App Store and Google Play. Veve sells only 3D image NFTs of major brands. For example, Veve features NFTs of *Ghostbusters*, *Batman*, *Back to the Future*, *Jurassic Park*, and *Star Trek: The Next Generation*.

You can manipulate the size and angle of the 3D images from the NFTs and place them in other apps, add them to photos, and share them on social media.

Pros

- High-quality 3D files
- NFTs of some popular brands
- Don't need cryptocurrency to buy NFTs

Cons

- You can't transfer your NFTs out of the Veve app.
- You can't sell Veve NFTs; you can only trade them for other NFTs.
- The user interface is a bit clunky.

Known Origin

Website: `Knownorigin.io`

Known Origin prides itself as an artist-driven marketplace, which is limited to NFTs of digital art. It features a primary marketplace of new art NFT drops and a secondary marketplace where collectors can sell NFTs they own.

Artists need to apply in order to create and sell NFTs on the marketplace. Know Origin tries "to ensure a very high level of due diligence" when selecting artists for the platform.

Pros

- High-quality art NFTs
- Elegant, user-friendly interface

Cons

- Fee of 15 percent of primary sales
- Currently not accepting new artist applications
- Based on the Ethereum blockchain, which can have high gas prices for transactions

Myth Market

Website: Myth.market

Myth Market focuses on trading card NFTs and is actually just a hub for five distinct markets:

- GPK.Market (Garbage Pail Kids trading cards)
- GoPepe.Market (trading cards featuring the Pepe meme)
- Heroes.Market (Blockchain Heroes trading cards)
- KOGS.Market (KOGS trading cards)
- Shatner.Market (trading cards featuring William Shatner)

Like Atomic Hub, Myth Market (and its submarkets) utilize the WAX blockchain.

Pros

- No ETH gas fees
- Environmentally friendly

Cons

- You can only buy and sell NFTs offered on each submarket.
- The WAX blockchain is much less popular than the ETH blockchain.
- NFTs are not transferable to the ETH blockchain.

Wrap-Up

Keep in mind that there are dozens of NFT marketplaces. The NFT space is evolving rapidly, and new marketplaces will pop up, while others will fade into obscurity or simply cease to exist.

You can find links to the previous marketplaces and several others, on the book's Resources page at `TheNFThandbook.com/Resources`, which we will keep updated.

Now that you have a sense of the NFT market, let's start creating your first NFT.

CHAPTER

6

Creating and Minting NFTs

In this chapter, we'll go through, step by step, creating an NFT and minting it (putting it on the blockchain) from scratch. Even if you're a complete noob, you can do it. No prior NFT, blockchain, or technical experience is necessary. So, get ready to join the NFT craze.

The main steps for doing this are as follows:

- Creating the main content and other aspects of your NFT
- Creating a cryptocurrency wallet (specifically a MetaMask wallet)
- Creating an account on OpenSea (the largest NFT marketplace)
- Creating a collection on OpenSea
- Minting your NFT on OpenSea

To keep the process as simple as possible, let's focus on creating a digital art NFT, the most popular type of NFT.

Creating the Aspects of Your NFT

The first step is to create all of the aspects of your NFT. NFTs can have all of the following aspects, as covered in Chapter 2, "What Are NFTs?":

- Main content
- Name
- Preview content
- Description
- Traits
- Unlockable content
- Perks
- Ongoing royalty
- Supply
- External link

We'll go through each, one by one, but not in that order.

Main Content

This is the first and foremost step to creating your NFT, as the main content is the heart of your NFT.

Projects such as Meebits use images of 3D characters as their main content, with buyers able to unlock the actual 3D files once they own the Meebit (more on unlockable content later). Created by the people at Larva Labs, known for CryptoPunks, Meebits are 20,000 artificial intelligence (AI)–generated characters with varying rarities. The idea behind Meebits is for people to use these characters as avatars in virtual worlds, video games, and virtual reality (VR). So, owners unlock an OBJ file allowing them to import the character into animation and modeling software. But the main content is a simple image that people can use to show off their collection.

It can be daunting to look at headline-grabbing projects such as Meebits and think, "I can't possibly create something as visually appealing as this." But don't fret; you can keep it simple and just take a picture or video with your phone or use an image or video from your phone's photo gallery.

If you're feeling creative, you can make a piece of digital art. If you like to draw or use traditional materials, feel free to do that and then scan (or take a picture of) your artistic creation to make a digital file.

If you'd like to create a work of digital art in a digital medium, you can use these free software programs, websites, and apps:

- Krita (`Krita.org`), downloadable software for Mac, PC, and Linux
- Infinite Painter app for iOS and Android
- `Bomomo.com`, a website for creating abstract art
- `Pixelart.com`, a website for creating pixel art

We don't have any particular recommendations. Try them out. Matt did (see Figure 6.1). For other options, visit the Resources page of *The NFT Handbook* website: `TheNFThandbook.com/Resources`.

As far as the dimensions of your photo or artwork go, any size should be fine. But note that larger would be better than smaller, so the image can be displayed on large screens. However, it's not an absolute requirement. The image should be as high resolution as possible, but keep in mind that marketplaces have a file size limit. We'll be minting your NFT on OpenSea, which allows a maximum file size of 40 MB.

FIGURE 6.1   Abstract art image Matt created with Bomomo

For video, the quality should be at least HD, but keep it relatively short to stay within the maximum file size limit.

If you have a specific idea for an image but don't have artistic talent, you can hire someone to bring it to life. A couple of good sites to check out for that are `Fiverr.com` and `Upwork.com`.

Sometimes, the main content of the NFT is in the unlockable content, in which case you will still need an image for the NFT. For example, Matt created an NFT of a short story he wrote for an assignment in 8th grade. The story is in the unlockable content, and the main image is the cover he drew for the story.

If you're planning to use the image or likeness of someone famous, there may be some legal issues associated with that. Also, do not just grab any image off the Internet for your main content because that could be a copyright infringement. For a thorough discussion of these and other potential issues, see Chapter 9, "Legal Aspects of NFTs."

Name

This is pretty straightforward. Once you have your main content, what would you like to call your NFT?

The name of your NFT is essential and shouldn't be overlooked, as it's the first way to stand out in the crowded marketplace. When Sarah Meyohas got into NFTs in 2015, the conceptual artist made an instant splash with the name of her work: *Bitchcoin*. In an interview with Yahoo Finance, Sarah describes Bitchcoin as "an artwork, a sincere funding model introducing blockchain, tokenization, and a satirical prediction of meme-ification into the realm of fine art." Six years later, these trends have become impossible to ignore.

Bitchcoin was created as a currency that collectors could use to redeem for Sarah's physical artworks in her collection "Cloud of Petals" or to hold as an investment. Today, cryptocurrency and NFT collectors have proven Sarah correct, gravitating toward anything ironic or "meme-ified" in this space. And the Bitchcoin play on words has seen a big lift from collectors because the name catches your attention, while the artwork and story add substance.

For the purposes of this chapter, we're going to create a unique 1 of 1 NFT. If you like, you could put "(1 of 1)" in the name, although it's certainly not necessary. Usually, this would be done in a collection to distinguish it from other NFTs that are part of a series (have multiple editions), for example, *(1-of-1) GRONK Career Highlight Card*.

If you plan to make more than one edition of your NFT, then you could put "(x of x)" in the name, for example, *Julian Edelman INCREDELMAN XLIX (14/30)*. We usually see the "(x of x)" or "(x/x)" at the end of the name, particularly if it's a multi-edition NFT, but at the beginning is fine too.

Preview Content

If you're using an image or GIF as your main content, there will be no separate preview content. However, if you would like to use an audio or video file as your main content, you will need to create an image (or GIF) as your preview content. Just follow the steps listed earlier. Ideally, the preview image would relate somehow to the audio or video file. Generally, a frame from a video would be used as the preview image.

Perks

As discussed earlier, perks are not technically an aspect of the NFT but are designed to incentivize someone to buy the NFT and increase the NFT's value.

Gary Vaynerchuk, for example, has built his entire collection of VeeFriends around perks. With a total of 10,255 NFTs, he's broken down the rarity of his NFTs based on the perks of owning one. For example, 9,400 of the "admission token" VeeFriends give owners admission to his VeeCon conference for the next three years, and 555 of the "gift token" VeeFriends grant owners a minimum of six physical gifts sent to them each year for the next three years. And at the rarest level, 300 "access token" VeeFriends come with varying levels of personal access to Gary V, including a bowling session, group brainstorming sessions, and one-on-one advising.

Perks can be anything. Just make sure it's something that you have the right to deliver (it doesn't belong to someone else) and that it's already in your possession. You don't want to be in a situation where you promise to deliver something that you don't have.

An important note about perks: You usually don't want to provide the perk to every future owner of the NFT, and you can't if it's a unique item. That's why perks are often limited to the first buyer, such as the highest bidder of the initial auction. Or, you could say that the perk will go to whoever owns the NFT on a specific date. For example, the perks of VeeFriends are mostly redeemable every year for three years, and they define the year clearly as starting May 6th, when the project was released. VeeFriends owners must take an additional step of verifying their ownership of the NFT, at which point the number of perks redeemed is tracked clearly, so that the perk can't be used more than as specified.

Of course, you can provide the perk to every future owner of the NFT if you like. We just don't recommend it because it could get out of hand quickly if the NFT is transacted frequently.

Unlockable Content

Is there any content that you would like to provide that only the owner of the NFT can access? As discussed in Chapter 2, it could be any type of content, such as an image, a video, a PDF file, login credentials for a website, your email address, or just some words of wisdom.

As mentioned, each Meebit comes with an OBJ file as its unlockable content. But if you recall from Chapter 2, the unlockable content in the NFT can be text only. So, if you're providing an actual file (image, video, and so on), then you will need to store that file securely somewhere on the Internet and provide a link to the file. Ideally, the file would be password protected, so not just anyone can access it. After all, as unlockable content, it should be available only to the owner of the NFT.

If you're offering perks, you must include in the unlockable content information how the buyer can access the perks. If the perk is a physical item, include your email address with a note for the owner to email you and that you will email (or snail mail) them the perks. You can also do the same for unlockable content; that you will email them the file or a link to the file. We recommend not using your primary email address for this, but instead, you should set up a different email address specifically for this purpose. You don't want your primary email address floating around forever, and you don't want the buyer or any future buyers constantly emailing you.

Note that it's your responsibility to deliver the unlockable content and perks and ensure that the unlockable content remains available for the owner, and future owners of the NFT. If you're not willing to take on this responsibility, do not include any unlockable content or perks.

Description

This is also pretty straightforward. You want to describe your NFT. Some people keep it short and sweet, while others like to give a lot of detail. In fact, you don't even need to provide a description at all.

Here are some tips for describing your NFT:

- If your NFT is a 1 of 1, then mention that. Use words like "unique" or "one of a kind." Although implied, you could also note for extra emphasis that the NFT will never be minted again. If the NFT is part of an edition, mention the edition number and total number of NFTs in the edition. For example, "This NFT is number 5 in an edition of 30." Or you could say, for example, "This NFT is limited to 30 editions. Each edition is sequentially numbered." You could also add "No further editions will be minted."

- If you're offering perks, these must be spelled out in the description. Be as clear and precise as possible. You don't want any misunderstanding about what you're offering. Also, as discussed, if the perks are limited to the first buyer, you must be clear about that. For example, the (1-of-1)

GRONK Career Highlight Card NFT states, "In addition to winning the Career Highlight NFT card, the highest bidder of this auction will be awarded...." It might be better to be even more precise. Instead of "this auction," it may be preferable to say, "the initial auction." Note, this is not intended to be legal advice. You just want to be as precise as possible so that no issues arise later.

- Also, as discussed, alternatively, you may want to add a date such that only the owner of the NFT on that date can redeem the perks. Since the NFT could be transferred on that date, there could technically be two (or more) owners on that date. So, be more precise and include a time with the date, and also state the time zone. For example, "Must be holding this NFT at 12:00 pm EST May 8, 2021, to redeem this offer."

- If you have unlockable content, you can mention what it is in the description or keep it a complete surprise. We suggest mentioning what the content is, particularly if it will add value to the NFT and pique the curiosity of potential buyers.

Sometimes, the unlockable content is the main content of the NFT, for example, if you wrote a poem or a short story for your NFT. In such a case, you would certainly want to mention it in the description.

Ongoing Royalty

This feature allows you, the NFT creator, to earn from future sales of your NFT. Every time your NFT is sold (at least on the marketplace on which it was created), you will receive a certain percentage of those sales. And you can choose the royalty percentage.

Note that if the percentage you choose is too high, that's going to be a disincentive for future owners of your NFT to sell it. Let's say, for example, you choose a royalty of 50 percent. If someone buys your NFT for one ETH, then that person would have to sell it for at least two ETH to make any profit. And the marketplace is going to charge a percentage as well.

We recommend a royalty of 10 percent, but you're free to charge whatever you like.

Supply

Like the vast majority of NFTs, the supply of your NFT should be 1. This will simplify the NFT creation process, won't dilute the value of your NFT, and will streamline the process of selling your NFT.

External Link

On OpenSea, you can provide a link that will appear on your NFT's detail page. The link should lead to a web page with more detail about the NFT. For example, if there's a great story behind the NFT and it's too long to fit in the description, you can put the full story on a separate web page. You can link to any page, really, but it should be related to the NFT.

The external link is entirely optional. If there's no relevant page to which you can link, that's fine—no need to include one.

Creating a Cryptocurrency Wallet

If you're not already on the blockchain, this is the exciting part of getting onto the blockchain and entering the world of cryptocurrencies. To create your NFT, you're going to need a cryptocurrency wallet. More specifically, you're going to need an Ethereum wallet, in which you can hold ETH, ERC20 tokens, and NFTs. There are other blockchains that support NFTs, but we're going to focus on Ethereum, the most popular NFT blockchain.

Creating a MetaMask Wallet

There are several different Ethereum wallets to choose from, but we're going to use MetaMask, the most popular wallet and easiest to use. It works as an extension to your browser: Chrome, Firefox, or Brave. So, you'll need to be using one of those browsers to continue. Please download and install one of those browsers if you do not have any of them. Links are available on the book's Resources page at TheNFThandbook.com/Resources. Also, note that all links mentioned throughout the book are available on the Resources page.

You can also use the MetaMask wallet on your phone, either iOS or Android. But since we will be minting an NFT, we recommend doing it on a computer. So, if your main content is on your phone, make sure to transfer it to your computer.

1. The first step is to go to MetaMask.io using one of the three browsers mentioned (see Figure 6.2).

2. From there, click the **Download** or **Download Now** button. You should arrive at a page similar to the one shown in Figure 6.3.

3. Click the **Install MetaMask** button. Your browser's name will appear on the button as well. Note that if you're using the Brave browser, the button may say Install MetaMask for Chrome. It's OK to click and continue with Brave.

4. On the next page, click the + **Add to Firefox** button, **Add to Chrome** button, or **Add to Brave** button.

   Your browser will prompt you whether you want to add the MetaMask extension. Click **Add** or **Add extension**.

5. On the next page, click the **Get Started** button. You should arrive at a page similar to the one shown in Figure 6.4.

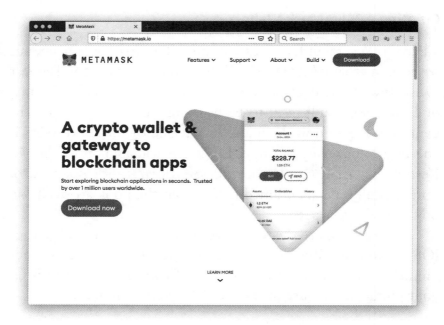

FIGURE 6.2 MetaMask home page

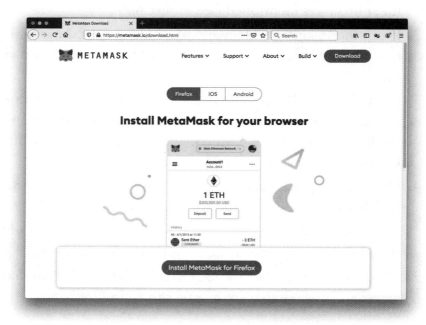

FIGURE 6.3 MetaMask download page

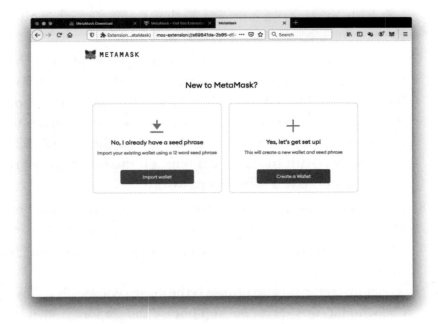

FIGURE 6.4 New to MetaMask? page

On this page, you can import an existing MetaMask wallet. So, after you create your MetaMask wallet, if you would like to use it on a different browser or device, you would click the **Import wallet** button. Of course, you can also create a new MetaMask wallet on a different browser or device, in which case you would have more than one Meta-Mask wallet, which is fine.

For now, since this will be your first MetaMask wallet, click the **Create a Wallet** button.

6. On the next page, you can choose whether you'd like to share anonymized data with MetaMask to help them improve the wallet's usability and user experience. Either selection is acceptable.

7. On the next page, you will need to create a password. Obviously, you should make one that no one will be able to figure

out. Either memorize it or write it down and store it in a safe. Do not store your password on your computer.

Note that this password will be specifically for the browser and device that you are currently using. If you import your MetaMask wallet to a different browser or device, you will need to create a new password specific to that browser/device. So, although it will be the same Meta-Mask wallet (with the same content) on the other browser/device, it will have a different password.

8. Click and review the terms of use. Afterward, select the box indicating that you have read and agree to the terms of use.

9. Click the **Create** button. You should arrive at a page similar to the one shown in Figure 6.5.

The secret backup phrase is the key to your wallet. Anyone who has this secret backup phrase can import your wallet into their browser (see step 5) and transfer out (steal) all of

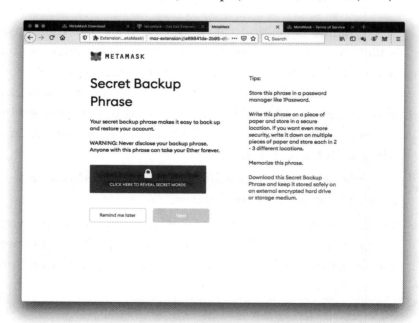

FIGURE 6.5   MetaMask Secret Backup Phrase page

your cryptocurrency and NFTs. In Chapter 3, "Why NFTs Have Value," we discussed some common scams to be wary of—it was not an exhaustive list. Scammers will try to get you to reveal your backup phrase. Do not do it. Do *not* reveal your backup phrase to anyone at any time.

The Importance of Your Backup Phrase

Never disclose your backup phrase.

Also, it's vitally important that you *do not lose* the backup phrase. If you lose your computer, it crashes, or you're no longer able to access it for whatever reason, the only way you can access your wallet is to import your backup phrase (see step 5) on a different device. If you lose or cannot access your backup phrase, then you will not be able to access your wallet, and all of your cryptocurrency and NFTs will be gone. Well, they actually won't be gone; you just won't be able to transfer them or sell them.

There are also some tips on this page. Let's address each one:

- We recommend that you *do not* store this phrase in a password manager like 1Password. If someone can access your password manager, your wallet is toast.
- We *do* recommend that you write the backup phrase on a piece of paper and store it in a secure location. A secure place is not a desk drawer. A secure location must be a safe or vault—someplace for which a key, combination, passcode, or biometric reading is required. Also, the page suggests that if you want even

(Continued)

(Continued)

more security, write the backup phrase down on multiple pieces of paper and store each in two or three different locations.

As mentioned, these locations must be secure. Note that multiple locations make your backup phrase more secure against losing it but less secure against theft—the more places that the phrase is located, the more places that can be compromised.

- Memorize the backup phrase. We feel that this is optional. Some people may find it challenging to memorize 12 random words, although creating a mnemonic might help. For example, "My very educated mother just served us nine pies" is a mnemonic for the planets in the solar system (assuming Pluto is still a planet). Do not solely rely on memorizing the backup phrase because if for some reason you cannot remember it 100 percent, you'll be out of luck if you need it.

- We do not recommend that you download the backup phrase, but you may keep it stored safely on an external encrypted hard drive or storage medium. Let us elaborate. Encrypted hard drives, flash drives, and other storage media are suitable for storing your backup phrase, but only if the drive or other storage media is encrypted. You can also keep your backup phrase on your computer in a password-protected folder, which is technically a mountable drive. For detailed instructions on how to do this, please refer to the book's resources page at TheNFThandbook .com/Resources. Rather than downloading the phrase directly to your computer, we recommend mounting an encrypted drive or password-protected folder, opening TextEdit or Notepad, cutting and pasting or typing in your backup phrase, and saving the text file in the encrypted drive or password-protected folder.

Now that you're aware of the gravity of the backup phrase, click **CLICK HERE TO REVEAL SECRET WORDS** on the MetaMask site. Write down the words (following the previous recommendations). Know that the order of the words matters, so make sure to write them down in order. Click **Next**.

10. On this page, click each word of your backup phrase in order. If you make a mistake, you can rearrange the words in the box by clicking and dragging. Click **Confirm** when done.

11. On the next page, again heed the warnings. Finally, when finished reading, click **All Done**.

    You may see a pop-up about swapping. Do not start swapping now—you can always do that later. We will cover swapping in Chapter 8. For now, close the pop-up.

That's it. Congratulations. You've just created a MetaMask wallet.

About Your MetaMask Wallet

You should now be on a page similar to Figure 6.6.

Your Address. If you click **Account 1** toward the top of the page, your address will be copied to the clipboard. This is your

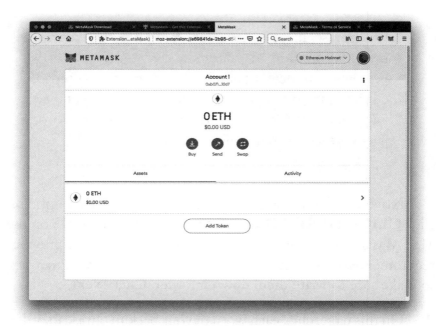

FIGURE 6.6 MetaMask wallet

public address. Think of it like a regular (snail mail) address. If someone were to mail you a check, you would give them the address to where they should mail it. Similarly, if someone were to send you ETH, an ERC20 token, or an NFT, you would first send them your MetaMask wallet address, the place to where they would send the ETH, tokens, or NFTs.

As we discussed in Chapter 3, you can enter your address into a block explorer such as Etherscan.io or Ethplorer.io to see all the contents of the address and all transactions to and from the address. Anyone with your address can see this information, which is fine; it's just part of the transparency of the blockchain.

Click the three dots to the right of **Account 1** and select **Account Details**. A pop-up will show your full 42-character address as well as the QR code for your address. Most mobile wallets can scan a QR code address rather than having to cut and paste the address and send it to someone.

You can also change the name of the account in the pop-up by clicking the pencil icon. Click the check mark to save your changes. It's not necessary to name your account, but doing so may be helpful if you'll be using multiple accounts in the wallet. Why would you need multiple accounts? For example, if you want to have more than one account on a particular NFT marketplace, you will need an address for each account. Or, you might want one address for NFTs and another address for cryptocurrency trading. There's no right or wrong reason, and you can create multiple addresses.

To create an additional address, click the circle in the upper right of the page, and then click **Create Account**. Enter a name for the account if you like, and then click **Create**. That's it. You can toggle between accounts by clicking the circle in the upper-right corner again.

A note about using your address: always cut and paste it (or use the QR code). Never type out your address, especially for someone who will be sending you cryptocurrency or an NFT. If you make a mistake on just one of the numbers or letters, you won't receive what they're sending.

The remainder of the wallet shows your assets (how much ETH and other tokens you have in your wallet), their current value, and activity (transactions in and out of the wallet). Note that each account in your wallet has different assets and activity.

Note that, technically, NFTs and cryptocurrency are not stored "in" your MetaMask wallet. Instead, they are stored on the Ethereum blockchain. Each blockchain asset (NFT, cryptocurrency token) has an associated address. The blockchain assets that you own are associated with an address that's in your wallet.

Accessing Your MetaMask Wallet.   To access your MetaMask wallet, click the fox icon in the upper-right corner of your browser. If you don't see it there, click the puzzle piece icon in the upper-right corner and then click **MetaMask** in the list of extensions. We recommend pinning the MetaMask icon to the browser for easier access. First, click the puzzle piece icon to bring up the list of extensions. Then, click the pushpin icon to the right of MetaMask on the list of extensions. If you're using Firefox, the fox icon should automatically be pinned to your browser.

If you use your wallet frequently, it will remain active. After a certain period of time, you will need to enter your password to regain access to the wallet. If you want to log out of the wallet, click the circle in the upper-right corner of the wallet, and click the **Lock** button right below the circle. We highly recommend logging out of (locking) your wallet if you share your computer with others or there are others around who could access your computer. If your wallet is not locked, anyone using your computer can transfer all your crypto and NFTs.

Creating an OpenSea Account

OpenSea is the largest NFT marketplace. In our opinion, it is also the most user-friendly. Additionally, there are no gas fees required to mint NFTs, although you will need to pay some gas fees the first time that you list NFTs for sale. We'll cover the listing of NFTs for sale in the next chapter.

1. Using the browser with which you created your MetaMask wallet, go to OpenSea.io. On the home page, click the **Create** button or click the profile icon in the upper-right corner and click **My Profile**.

2. On the next page, you'll be asked to sign in to your wallet. Click the **Sign In** button. Your MetaMask wallet should open (see Figure 6.7).

3. Your account should already be checked. Click the **Next** button. The wallet will then notify you that you will be

FIGURE 6.7   Connecting MetaMask to OpenSea

allowing OpenSea to view the addresses of your permitted accounts, which is required. Click the **Connect** button. You should now be on a page similar to the one shown in Figure 6.8.

Congratulations. You now have an OpenSea account. If you're going to be selling NFTs, you should add a profile picture and banner image. Click the circle to upload a profile picture; 350 × 350 pixels are the preferred dimensions.

Click the pencil icon in the upper-right corner to upload a banner image. Shoot for dimensions of around 1400 × 400. Note that the banner will look different depending on your device and the width of your browser window. OpenSea suggests avoiding

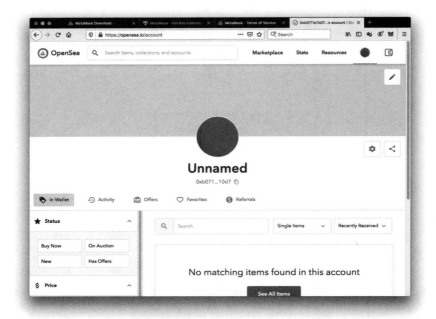

FIGURE 6.8   OpenSea account page

text in your banner. Also, keep the important part of the image in the vertical center because that's the part of the banner that will always show.

To name your account, click the gear icon at the right. This will open your MetaMask wallet, asking you to click the **Sign** button. By doing so, you are agreeing to the OpenSea terms of service. This is also a security mechanism. Only the person who has access to your MetaMask wallet (you) can access the settings in your OpenSea account. If your MetaMask wallet is locked, enter your password to unlock it. Note that you will not be creating an OpenSea password or other login credentials, as your MetaMask wallet serves the purpose of protecting your account.

On the General Settings page, enter a username to be associated with your account. You can also add a bio. We recommend that you do so. Tell the world your remarkable story. Finally, enter your email address and click the **Save** button when done.

You should then receive an email from OpenSea. Click **VERIFY MY EMAIL** in the email you receive, and you're done.

To access your account info, click your profile picture in the upper-right corner on any page on OpenSea.

Creating a Collection

All NFTs on OpenSea are held in *collections*, which are groups of similarly themed NFTs. There are tons of collections on OpenSea, such as CryptoPunks, F1 Delta Time, Rob Gronkowski Championship Series NFTs, Decentraland Wearables, Official Three Stooges NFTs, Ksoids, and thousands of others. A collection is like a storefront. So, before you can create an NFT on OpenSea, you must first create a collection. Even if you're making just one NFT, it still sits in a collection.

This section will walk you through how to create a collection on OpenSea. But before we do that, you should first complete the elements of your collection.

Elements of a Collection

There is certain content and other information that you will need for your collection:

- Theme or subject matter
- Name
- Logo
- Banner image
- Featured image
- Description
- Links
- Ongoing royalty
- Ongoing royalty address

Let's discuss each, one at a time.

Theme or Subject Matter.   Most collections have a particular theme or subject matter to which all of the NFTs in the collection relate. For example, the "Rob Gronkowski Championship Series NFTs" collection not surprisingly contains NFTs representing one or all of Rob Gronkowski's four NFL championships. Also, the "CryptoPunks" collection contains, you guessed it, just CryptoPunk NFTs.

What do you want to make NFTs of? What are some of your favorite subjects? You don't need to get too fancy or deeply meaningful with your theme or subject matter; it's just something that ties all of the NFTs together. You could also just have an assortment of NFTs. There are no rules with respect to a theme or subject matter.

Say, for example, you're really into two distinct subjects, such as classic cars and dolphins. It probably wouldn't make sense to put NFTs of both into one collection. The answer would simply be to create two separate collections: one for classic car NFTs and one for dolphin NFTs. In fact, you can have multiple collections in your OpenSea account. So, any time you come up with a new theme or subject, you can simply create a new collection by repeating the steps in this section.

Name.   Ideally, the collection's name should identify the collection's theme or subject matter, as in the earlier Gronk and CryptoPunks examples. Feel free to get more creative, but try to avoid confusion or a disconnect between the name and subject matter. If your collection has no particular theme or subject matter, you could always name it something like "Matt's NFT Collection" or "QuHarrison's Awesome NFTs."

Logo.   You'll need to create a logo for your collection; 350×350 are the recommended dimensions. What visual represents your collection or its theme? You could use part of an image from one of your NFTs, your profile picture, your company logo, or any other interesting visual. We suggest poking around OpenSea to see what other collections are doing. Pay attention to other collections' banner images and descriptions as well.

Banner Image.   Although it's optional, we highly recommend that you create a banner image for your collection. A blank (gray) banner area expresses an attitude of unprofessionalism. Especially if you want to sell NFTs, you need to have a catchy banner image.

Shoot for the same dimensions (1400×400) as your profile banner image. This image's appearance will also change depending on the device and browser width. As with the logo, use a visual that complements the theme or subject of the collection. It can even be similar to (or an extended version of) the collection's logo image. For example, see Figure 6.9.

Featured Image.   The featured image is an image that OpenSea may use to feature your collection on the home page, category pages, or other promotional areas of OpenSea. We highly recommend creating one because you never know—OpenSea may feature you, which would drive significant traffic to your collection.

The recommended dimensions for the featured image are 600×400. We suggest just repurposing your banner image to these dimensions. Not only will this likely be the easiest route, more importantly, it will provide consistent branding. When someone clicks the featured image to arrive at your collection, they'll know they arrived at the right place.

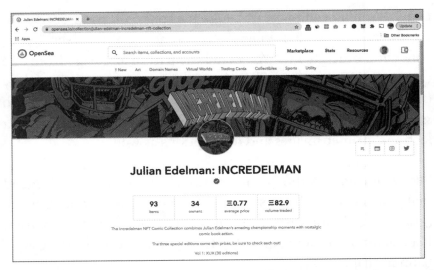

FIGURE 6.9 "Julian Edelman: INCREDELMAN" collection logo and banner images

Description.   Even though a description of your collection is also optional, we highly recommend writing one. Ideally, the description should provide information about the NFTs in the collection and entice potential buyers. There are no particular rules, but here are a few tips:

- Tell a story. What inspired you to create the NFTs?
- Describe the NFTs in the collection.
- Provide information about the artist. This could be background, influences, or anything of interest.
- If you have different editions of NFTs in the collection, list them and how many NFTs are in each edition.
- Describe any exciting perks or unlockable content.
- If the proceeds are going to a particular charity, mention it.
- You could indicate when the auction will end.
- Add any other interesting, relevant information.

This is not an exhaustive list. You certainly don't need to include all of these suggestions. Be as creative and detailed as you like. Just note that there's a 1,000-character limit.

You can use Markdown syntax in your description. This provides a way to have bold or italicized text and headings with larger text, among other features. For example, to make text bold, write it as such: `**bold text**`. For italicized text, use `*italicized text*`. For more information on Markdown syntax, visit the Resources page at `TheNFThandbook.com/Resources`.

Don't get hung up on making your collection elements perfect right now; they can all be changed later. Also, in Chapter 7, we'll provide tips on making your collection more marketable.

Links. On your collections page, you can link to your website and social media accounts. Specifically, you can provide links to your accounts on the following platforms:

- Discord
- Twitter
- Instagram
- Medium
- Telegram
- Your website

You can provide any, all, or none of the above links. If you have links for any of these platforms, we suggest you provide them. They allow potential buyers to learn more about you. The more they know, the more likely they'll buy. These links will help grow your social media followings as well. Additionally, these links may help OpenSea to verify your collection, which we'll discuss later in this chapter.

Ongoing Royalty. We discussed this earlier in the chapter as an aspect of an NFT, but technically on OpenSea, the royalty percentage is set in the collection settings and will apply to all NFTs in the collection. Therefore, if you would like to set different royalties for different NFTs, the NFTs would have to reside in different collections.

Ongoing Royalty Address. When you sell an NFT, the funds (usually ETH) are placed in your MetaMask wallet at the address associated with your account. However, for the ongoing royalties, you set an address to which the ongoing royalty payments will be sent. This can be your MetaMask wallet address or any other Ethereum address that supports ERC20 tokens.

Now that you've created and gathered all the content and information you need, you're ready to create a collection.

Creating the Collection

To create a collection, follow these steps:

1. Hover your cursor over your profile picture on any OpenSea page, and click **My Collections**. Then on the My Collections page, in the "Create new collection" box, click the **Create** button.

2. In the "Create your collection" pop-up (pictured in Figure 6.10), drag your logo to the Logo box to upload it. Then enter the name of your collection. Next, enter (or cut and paste) your description. When done, click the **Create** button.

Now you have a collection!

But you're not done yet. You need to add the remaining elements to your collection. Go to the My Collections page by

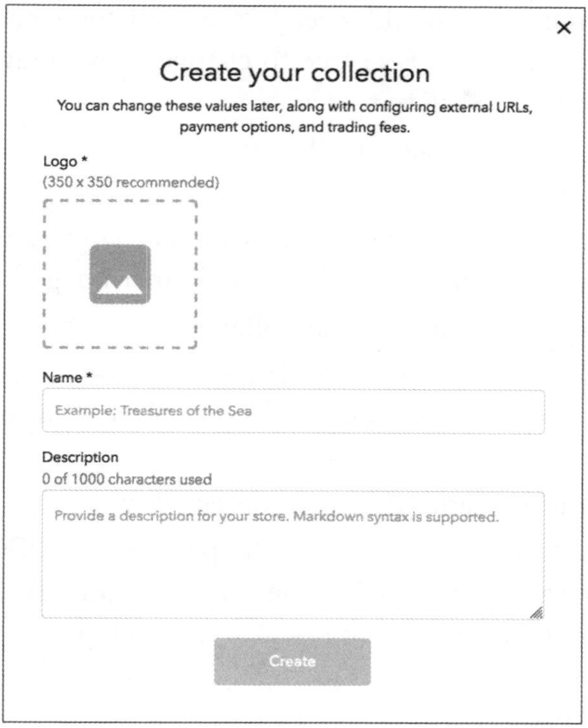

FIGURE 6.10 "Create your collection" pop-up

hovering your cursor over your profile picture and selecting My Collections. From the My Collections page, click the logo of the collection you created.

On your collection page, the first thing we're going to do is to add the banner image. Click the pencil icon in the upper-right corner of the page and locate the banner image file on your computer.

Next, click the **Edit** button below your description. You will arrive at the "Edit your collection" page, where you can add or change any element of your collection at any time.

Most of the information requested on this page is relatively straightforward, especially since you already have the content and other information prepared.

Logo Image: You should already see your logo image in the Logo image box. Feel free to change it by dragging a new logo image to the box.

Featured Image: Drag your featured image into the Featured Image box.

Banner Image: If you haven't already added your banner image, drag your banner image into the Banner image box.

Name: Enter the name of your collection.

URL: You can customize the URL (web address) of your collection. It should, but doesn't have to, be related to the name of the collection.

Description: Cut and paste your description.

Category: Adding a category will help make your NFTs discoverable on OpenSea. Click the **Add Category** button. There are five categories to choose from, as follows:

- Art
- Trading Cards
- Collectibles
- Sports
- Utility

   Select the one that's most relevant to what your NFTs will be.

Links: Enter your website address and social media links or handles for each particular platform that you use.

Royalties: Enter the royalty percentage. For a 10 percent royalty, enter 10, not .1. After you enter the percentage, an entry box will appear for your payout address. Cut and paste in your desired payout address.

Payment tokens: These are the cryptocurrencies with which someone can purchase your NFTs. You can include additional cryptocurrencies (ERC20 tokens) by clicking the **Add token** button and selecting them from the list. There's no real need to add other tokens unless there's a particular token you'd like to receive or are trying to promote.

Display theme: The display theme affects how your NFTs' main content is shown. If you're using PNG images with transparent backgrounds, then the Padded theme would probably be best. Otherwise, we recommend the Contained theme.

Explicit & sensitive content: If your content is not safe for work or contains pornography or explicit language, then toggle the switch on. If you're not sure, it's better to err on the side of caution.

Collaborators: If you're creating your NFTs together with someone else, you can add them as a collaborator. Click the **Add collaborator** button and enter their Ethereum address in the pop-up. Note that collaborators will have admin-like capabilities. They will be able to modify collection settings, receive payments for NFTs that they created, change the collection's royalty payout address, and create new items, so be careful who you add. At this point, to keep the process simple (and more secure), we recommend not adding any collaborators.

When you're done inputting everything, click the **Submit Changes** button. If the button is grayed out, either you left out some required information or content or you need to unlock your MetaMask wallet.

Your collection is complete (except for adding NFTs, which we'll cover in the next section).

Before moving on to the next section, you should review your collection. If you're still on the "Edit your collection" page, click the "< Back to [your collection name]" link in the upper-left corner; or, hover the cursor over your profile picture, select My Collections, and then click your collection's logo. You are now on your collection page. To see how others will view your collection page, click the **Visit** button below the description. Or, you could enter your collection's URL in your browser.

Make sure that everything looks good. Does the important part of your banner image appear? Is the description correct? If you used Markdown syntax, did those parts come out right? You should also notice your links in the upper-right corner. And, if you're just starting out, your stats will be all zero. These will automatically update as you accrue activity.

If you need to make changes, click the pencil icon in the upper-right corner. If not, you're ready to mint an NFT.

Verification

Before you start minting, a word about *verification*. You may have noticed that some collections have a blue check mark. For example, see Figure 6.11.

Like on other platforms, the blue check mark indicates that the collection is verified. It has been reviewed by OpenSea staff, who have verified that the collection owner is who they purport to be. This obviously gives buyers more comfort when bidding on and buying NFTs from the collection.

Akwasi Frimpong's The Rabbit Theory ✅

FIGURE 6.11 Akwasi Frimpong's The Rabbit Theory verified collection

Currently, you can't request verification for your collection on OpenSea. It's added to account pages only if the figure or company controlling the wallet is at risk of impersonation, which is usually reserved for collections created by high-profile public figures or organizations.

Most collections on OpenSea are not verified, so you shouldn't be concerned that your collection isn't either.

Minting an NFT

Back in the early days of NFTs, the only way to mint an NFT was by writing a smart contract. In essence, a *smart contract* is programming code that runs on the Ethereum network. Technically, the Ethereum network is the Ethereum Virtual Machine (EVM), a giant computer spread across multiple thousands of nodes around the world. A smart contract is basically a computer program written in Solidity, Ethereum's native programming language based on JavaScript.

After writing the smart contract, you would have to test it and then deploy it to the EVM. Testing is a crucial step because once deployed to the blockchain, there's no fixing it. Every NFT is a different contract, and, of course, there are gas fees every time you deploy a contract to the blockchain.

Today, with the advent of OpenSea and other NFT marketplaces, you don't have to write a smart contract, know how to code, know how to test it, or know how to deploy it. Matt has done some coding in his time and even learned some Solidity. So, we can attest to how vastly simpler it is to mint an NFT on OpenSea.

Since you've already created all the aspects of your NFT, the actual minting process is pretty straightforward. Let's get started.

On OpenSea, hover over your profile picture, select My Collections, and then click your collection's logo. Next, from your collections page, click the **Add New Item** button. You're now at the "Create new item page," as shown in Figure 6.12.

Image, Video, Audio, or 3D Model: This is where you upload your NFT's main content. Just drag it into the box. If you upload an audio or video file, a separate Preview Image box will appear. In this case, drop your preview image (or GIF) into the Preview Image box.

Name: Enter the name of your NFT.

External Link: Enter the external link for your NFT if you have one.

Description: Cut and paste in your NFT's description. You can use Markdown syntax here as well.

Properties, Levels, Stats: As discussed in Chapter 2, the Properties, Levels, and Stats fields are particularly useful for digital game trading card NFTs and in-game item NFTs. Unless there's a compelling reason or relevance to your NFT, we suggest just leaving them blank.

If you're creating multiple editions of an NFT, for example, one with 10 editions, where each NFT is sequentially numbered 1–10, some NFT creators will put the edition number in the Stats. This is not required, but if you would like to do this, click the + button to the right of Stats. In the pop-up, enter Edition as the name, then the NFT's edition number, and the total number of NFTs in the edition. Save it when you're done.

Unlockable Content: If you have unlockable content, toggle the switch on. Then cut and paste in your unlockable content. As discussed earlier, this must be text, no files. You can use Markdown syntax here as well.

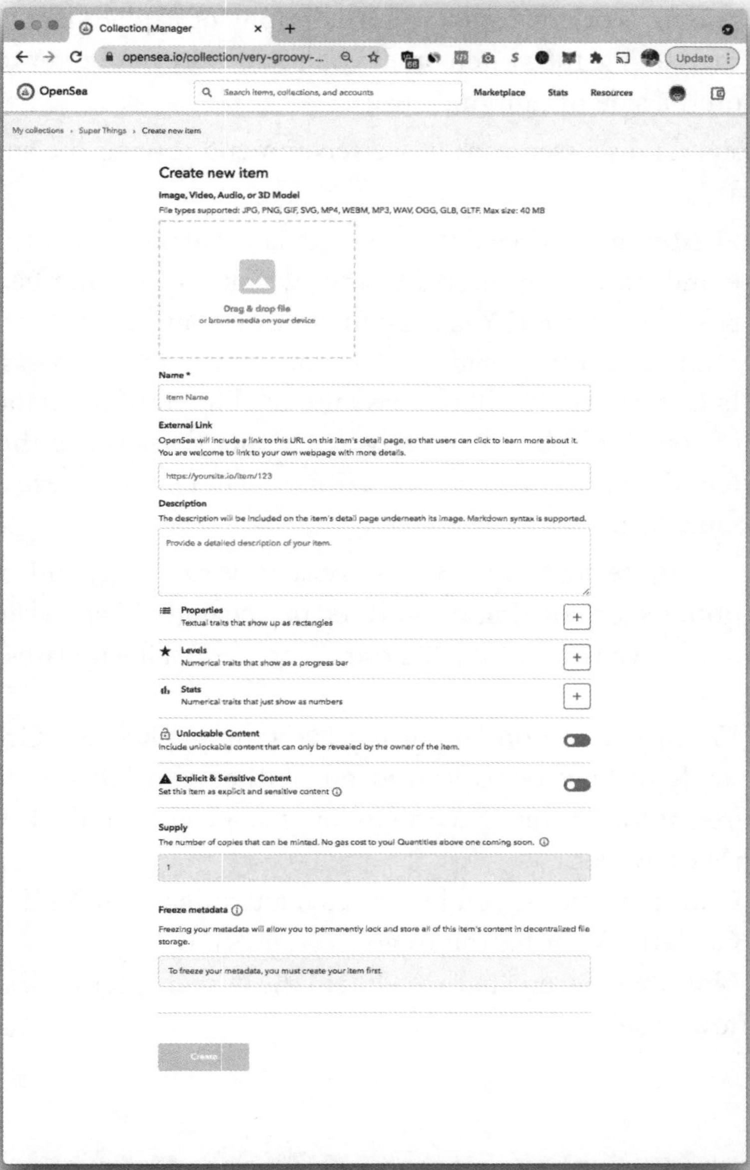

FIGURE 6.12 "Create new item" page

Explicit & Sensitive Content: If the content of your NFT is not safe for work or contains pornography or explicit language, then toggle the switch on. If you're not sure, it's better to err on the side of caution.

Supply: As discussed earlier, we recommend leaving the supply at 1.

Freeze Metadata: Freezing your metadata will permanently lock it and store it on the IPFS, after which you will not be able to edit your NFT. You must first create your item before you can freeze your metadata. You will also need to pay a gas fee. Is it worth it? It will increase the likelihood of permanence of your NFT, but it's up to you whether that's worth the gas fee. We suspect that most creators will not opt to freeze their metadata.

Note that OpenSea is constantly evolving, and some options for creating new NFTs may change. Please visit the book's website at TheNFThandbook.com for updates.

When you're done inputting everything, click the **Create** button. If the button is grayed out, either you left out some required information or content or you need to unlock your MetaMask wallet.

Congratulations, you just created and minted an NFT!

Click the **Visit** button to go to your NFT.

Now that you created an NFT, in the next chapter we'll show you how to sell it.

CHAPTER

7

Selling NFTs

In this chapter, we'll go through, step-by-step, how to sell the non-fungible tokens (NFTs) that you created. Since you made your NFTs on OpenSea, you'll be selling your NFTs there. To list your NFTs for sale on OpenSea, you're going to need some Ethereum to cover the gas fees. So, we're also going to walk you through how to open an account with a cryptocurrency exchange, how to fund that account, how to purchase ETH, and how to transfer the ETH to your MetaMask wallet. If you've never dealt with cryptocurrency before, don't worry. Soon it will be second nature.

Your Exchange Account

Listing your NFTs for sale on OpenSea requires some gas fees, which means that you'll need some Ethereum in your MetaMask wallet to cover the fees. Some exchanges require that you pay gas fees when you mint your NFTs. Even if you don't plan to create any NFTs, you'll generally need Ethereum (or some other cryptocurrency) if you plan to buy any NFTs.

NFTs are blockchain assets, and as such, they're mainly bought and sold with cryptocurrency. So, how do you get Ethereum and other cryptocurrencies? You do this on a cryptocurrency exchange. There are several reputable exchanges that you can use: Coinbase, Binance, Crypto.com, and Voyager, among others. Of these, we recommend Coinbase, especially if you're in the United States. So, we'll be using it as the example exchange in this chapter. But feel free to use another exchange if you like. You can find links to all of our recommended exchanges on the book's Resources page: TheNFThandbook.com/Resources.

So, let's get started. The first step is to create a Coinbase account.

Creating a Coinbase Account

Coinbase is an exchange where you can purchase some of the popular cryptocurrencies with dollars. You can also sell these cryptocurrencies for dollars, which you can then send to your bank.

In this section, we'll walk you through how to create a Coinbase account. If you already have a Coinbase account or an account on another exchange, you can skip this section. Note that you must be at least 18 years old to open a Coinbase account.

Before you create an account, make sure that you have all of the following:

- A government-issued photo ID
- A phone number connected to your smartphone (you'll receive SMS text messages)
- The latest version of your browser (Chrome is recommended).

Let's get started.

1. Go to `Coinbase.com` and click the **Get Started** button.
   In the popup, shown in Figure 7.1, enter your information,
   including a password. As discussed in the previous chapter,
   do not keep the password in a text file on your computer
   (unless it's on an encrypted drive). Write it down and store
   it in a secure place.

   Make sure to read the user agreement and privacy policy,
   and check the box certifying your agreement and that you are
   at least 18 years of age. Then click the **Create account** button.
   Coinbase will then send you a verification email.

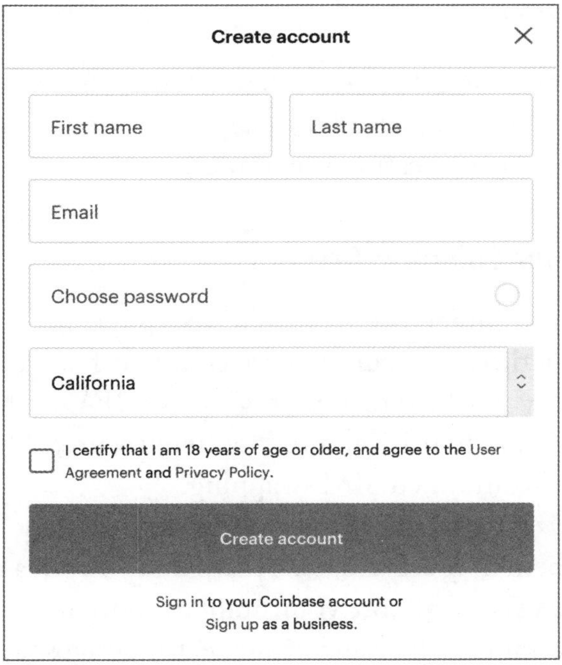

FIGURE 7.1 Coinbase "Create account" pop-up

2. In the email that you receive from Coinbase, click **Verify Email Address**. You'll be taken back to Coinbase, where you'll be asked to sign in.

3. Coinbase will prompt you to add a phone number. Select your country and enter your mobile phone number. Then click **Send Code**. Coinbase will text you a seven-digit code. Enter that code and click the **Submit** button.

4. On the next page, you'll need to enter your date of birth and address. You'll also have to answer a few questions and enter the last four digits of your Social Security number. Click the **Continue** button.

5. To buy, sell, send, and receive cryptocurrency, you'll need to verify your account. First, select the ID type that you would like to use. Then select an upload method and follow the instructions.

Verification usually takes a few minutes, but Coinbase may require time to conduct additional verification. Coinbase will email you when verification is complete.

Securing Your Coinbase Account

We highly recommend setting up a strong *two-factor authentication (2FA)* method to secure your account. When you signed up to Coinbase, you added text messaging as a 2FA method. Unfortunately, this method is only moderately secure. The reason is because of a scam called SIM swapping.

SIM swapping is where a scammer calls your mobile carrier, convinces them they are you, tells them that you got a new phone, and gets the carrier to port your number to their phone. In that case, the scammer will receive your text messages, among other things. If the scammer has your Coinbase password, they can now get into your Coinbase account and transfer out (steal) all of your cryptocurrency.

SIM swapping can cause severe damage. Just ask Michael Terpin, a renowned cryptocurrency enthusiast who sued AT&T over a SIM swap that resulted in a theft of nearly $24 million in cryptocurrency.

If you have a security key, you should use that for 2FA. Otherwise, we recommend Google Authenticator, which is easy and convenient while providing good security. Someone would need your actual physical phone (and your password, of course) to gain access to your Coinbase account.

1. If you don't already have the Google Authenticator app, download and install it on your smartphone from the App Store or Google Play store.

2. In Coinbase, click your name in the upper-right corner of the page, and then click **Settings** in the drop-down menu. On the Settings page, click **Security**. Click the **Select** button in the Authenticator area of the page.

    In the "Confirm settings change" pop-up, enter the code you receive via text message, and click the **Confirm** button. There will be a QR code on the "Enable Authenticator Support" pop-up.

3. Go to the Google Authenticator app on your phone. Tap the + sign and select **Scan a QR code**. Point your phone to your computer screen so that the Coinbase QR code fits within the green square. You should now see Coinbase listed in the Google Authenticator app, with six digits underneath. These six digits are your 2FA code.

Note that the digits change every 30 seconds, which enhances the security. Enter the six digits onto the "Enable Authenticator Support" pop-up before time runs out. If time does run out, just enter the new digits that appear. Then click the **Enable** button.

Now in the future, when you log into Coinbase, you'll be using the Google Authenticator app for 2FA.

Connecting Your Bank

To buy Ethereum and other cryptocurrencies, you're going to need to add a payment method. We recommend adding a bank account. The reason why we recommend this is so that you can later withdraw funds from Coinbase to your bank account after you sell cryptocurrency. If you're not comfortable connecting your bank account, you can purchase Ethereum with a credit card.

1. On Coinbase, go to the Settings page. From there, click Payment Methods. From there, click the **Add a payment method** button. In the "Add a payment method" pop-up, click Bank Account (or one of the other methods: PayPal, debit card, or wire transfer).

2. In the following pop-up, it should say that Coinbase uses Plaid (a third-party service) to link your bank. Click the **Continue** button.

    Select your bank from the list or search to find your bank.

3. Enter your user ID and password for your bank login. Don't worry. It's secure. Click the **Submit** button.

    You'll be asked how you want to verify your identity. Make a selection and click the **Continue** button.

4. Enter the code that you receive and click the **Submit** button.

    Select which bank account you would like to connect to Coinbase and click the **Continue** button. It should take about 30 seconds for Coinbase to verify and add your bank account.

Congratulations! Now you can buy cryptocurrency.

Buying Cryptocurrency

Now that you've connected your bank, you can buy some cryptocurrency. The first cryptocurrency you should buy is some Ethereum (ETH) to cover the necessary gas fees for listing your NFTs on OpenSea.

The first step is to figure out how much ETH to buy. On Coinbase, the purchases you make are in dollar amounts. In other words, you choose how many dollars' worth of ETH you want to buy. How much money you should spend on ETH depends on four factors:

- How much ETH you need
- The current gas prices
- The current price of ETH
- A comfortable buffer

Let's take each factor one at a time. First, listing on OpenSea requires two one-time gas fees; that is, one for each of the following transactions:

- To initialize your account for making sell orders, which needs to be done only once for your account
- To allow OpenSea to access your item (or all items in the collection, if the collection supports it) when a sale occurs

There's also a gas fee when you transfer the ETH from Coinbase to your MetaMask wallet. So, you're looking at three gas fees. But the gas fees aren't equal. Different types of transactions require different amounts of gas.

Regarding the gas fees for listing on OpenSea, depending on network congestion, we've seen it as low as $35 and as high as $812, which is quite a range. Note that that's the total for the two gas fees required by OpenSea. The gas fee for a simple ETH transaction, such as from Coinbase to your MetaMask wallet, is usually about 1/20 of that total, but it could be a little higher.

To get an estimate of the current gas fees, go to `etherscan .io/gastracker`. There you'll see the current gas prices and average transaction times for each price. Gas prices are listed in *gwei*, which is 0.000000001 ETH (see Figure 7.2).

The dollar value of the gas price shown is equal to the amount of gwei multiplied by the current value of Ethereum (which is the third factor listed earlier). The actual average gas price in Figure 7.2 for an ERC 20 token transfer will be between $2.98 (the amount stated in the Average box) and $9.21 (the amount listed in the Estimated Cost of Transfers & Interactions chart).

As a rule of thumb, to get a rough estimate of how much gas you'll need, take the former amount ($2.98 in this example) and multiply it by 20 to calculate how much ETH you'll need for OpenSea gas. Add the latter amount ($9.21 in this example) for the gas required to transfer the ETH from Coinbase to your MetaMask wallet. So, in this example, you would need approximately $2.98 × 20 + $9.21 = $68.81 worth of ETH to cover the gas fees.

Ethereum Gas Tracker

Mon, 24 May 2021 22:58:31 UTC

☺ Low	☺ Average	☺ High
42 gwei	**55 gwei**	**60 gwei**
$2.27 I ~ 11 mins:1 sec	$2.98 I ~ 30 secs	$3.25 I ~ 30 secs

Estimated Cost of Transfers & Interactions: View API

	Low	Average	High
⑦ ERC20 Transfer	$7.03	$9.21	$10.05
⑦ Uniswap Swap	$21.64	$28.34	$30.92
⑦ Uniswap Add/Remove LP	$18.94	$24.80	$27.05

FIGURE 7.2   Gas prices on Etherscan's Ethereum Gas Tracker

To obtain a more accurate amount of how much gas you'll need to list on OpenSea, we suggest going through the listing process, which is described in detail later in this chapter. During the listing process, you will be shown exactly how much gas is needed. Then return to this section on purchasing your Ethereum.

Finally, gas prices fluctuate and can spike up suddenly. On top of that, it may take a while to get the ETH to your MetaMask wallet. First, the transfer of funds from your bank could take a few days. Second, it's likely that your first transfer from Coinbase could take a few days because Coinbase usually puts a hold on initial transfers for security reasons to ensure that it's you making the transaction. Yes, these delays are hassles. But we put up with them because Coinbase is the most trusted and secure exchange.

The bottom line is that gas prices can be vastly different from when you went through the listing process and the time you received the funds in your MetaMask wallet. So, we recommend that you purchase at least twice the estimated amount, with a minimum of $250 of ETH. And even that amount could seriously fall short. Or, you could purchase $100 (or less) of ETH and just wait for gas prices to ease down before listing your NFTs.

If you're also going to be buying NFTs, then we suggest that you purchase a decent amount of ETH, as that will not only cover the necessary gas fees, but it will also enable you to buy some NFTs as well.

On your Coinbase dashboard, click the **Buy/Sell** button at the top. In the pop-up (see Figure 7.3), first select the cryptocurrency that you want to buy. Make sure to select Ethereum.

Then select a dollar amount or click the **Custom** box to enter a specific amount. If you entered a custom amount, click the **Preview Buy** button.

Review the amounts and make sure that you're buying ETH. Coinbase does charge a small fee, which will slightly reduce the

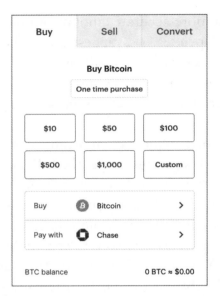

FIGURE 7.3   Coinbase "Buy" pop-up

amount of ETH you'll receive. Note that the fees don't scale proportionately. This means that the fees are a greater percentage of a smaller purchase and a much smaller percentage of a larger purchase. So keep in mind that fees-wise, it's always better to make a larger purchase. In any case, we don't recommend purchasing less than $50 worth.

If all looks good, click the **Buy now** button. It could take a few minutes for the transaction to complete.

Congratulations! You're now officially in the crypto space.

Funding Your MetaMask Wallet

Now that you've bought some Ethereum, it's time to transfer it to your MetaMask wallet. Please pay close attention to this section. If you make a mistake when moving cryptocurrency, it could be costly. You could potentially lose the amount that you sent. But don't worry. As long as you pay close attention, you should be fine. And soon, transferring cryptocurrency will be second nature.

1. Log in to Coinbase.
2. Open your MetaMask wallet, and click the wallet address at the top, right under the wallet's account name. (Please refer to Figure 6.6 in Chapter 6, "Creating and Minting NFTs.") Your ETH address should now be copied to your computer's clipboard.

    Open TextEdit, Notepad, or any other text editing software, and paste your address there. Ensure that the beginning and end of your address exactly match what's shown in your MetaMask wallet.
3. Go back to Coinbase. From the home page, click the **Send/Receive** button in the upper-right corner. The **Send** pop-up will appear (see Figure 7.4).

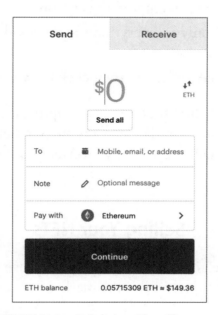

FIGURE 7.4 Coinbase "Send" pop-up

First, notice the **Pay with** section of the pop-up. If Ethereum is not indicated there, click in the **Pay with** section and select Ethereum.

4. Paste your address in the **To** section of the **Send** pop-up. Make sure that it matches the address that you pasted into your text editor exactly.

Next, enter the dollar amount of ETH that you want to send. Note that your account's ETH balance is shown at the bottom of the pop-up. When ready, click the **Continue** button.

5. Review all the following information carefully:
   ○ The amount you're sending
   ○ The address you're sending to
   ○ The currency you're sending

Note that the amount stated here may not be exactly what you entered. This is because the price of ETH has changed since you entered the amount.

If, and only if, everything looks good, click the **Send now** button.

6. Enter the 2FA code, and then click the **Confirm** button.

If this is your first time sending cryptocurrency from Coinbase, they may put an initial delay on the transaction. Otherwise, the ETH will usually appear in your MetaMask wallet within 10 minutes.

Selling Your NFTs

Now that you've got everything set up and have your MetaMask wallet funded, it's time to test the market and sell your NFTs.

Ways to Sell Your NFT

On OpenSea, there are three ways that you can sell an NFT.

- Leave it open for offers
- Set a price
- Start an auction

You can also group NFTs and sell them as a bundle. There's no best way to sell your NFTs; it's really up to how you would like to do it.

Leaving an NFT Open for Offers. Many NFT creators who aren't sure how to price their NFTs and aren't ready to do an auction will simply leave their NFTs open for offers. This means that anyone can make an offer on any of their NFTs. The NFT creator (or the current owner) can choose to accept the offer or not.

This is an excellent way to test the market by seeing how the market values the NFTs. But don't just sit back and expect offers to come rolling in. That's not going to happen if no one knows about your NFTs. You still have to market your NFTs if you want to make some sales. (See the section "Marketing Your NFTs" later in this chapter.)

Note that offers on OpenSea usually expire after 10 days and can be canceled anytime by the person who made the offer. So, if you like the offer, don't delay. You should receive an email from OpenSea every time someone makes an offer on an NFT you own.

Once you mint an NFT, it is automatically on the market since, after all, OpenSea is a marketplace. So, you don't have to do anything to allow others to make offers on your NFTs.

Setting a Price.   Rather than passively waiting for offers, if you have a price in mind for your NFT, you can list it for that price. Anyone can purchase the NFT by paying the price you set. Note that people can make offers for less than the price, and you are free to accept any such offer.

What's a reasonable price to set? It's hard to say because NFTs are unique, which is one reason for their soaring popularity. For example, when selling a house, the price is often determined by recent sales of comparable homes (similar size, same neighborhood, and so forth). If your NFT is part of a series of NFTs, such as a CryptoKitty, you could then use recent sales of other similar CryptoKitties to help determine a reasonable price to set for your NFT.

But if you have a unique piece of art, then finding comparables becomes more abstract. In this case, price, as in most markets, is based upon supply and demand. Is the NFT a "1 of 1," or are there multiple editions? A "1 of 1" would be more valuable.

Next, you'll have to gauge the potential demand for your NFT. How big is your following? How excited can you get them about your NFTs? What kind of marketing and promotion will you be doing? (See the section "Marketing Your NFTs" later in this chapter.)

Also, consider the value of any perks or unlockable content that you included with the NFT.

As you can see, pricing is more of an art than a science, particularly when you're starting out. Just make your best estimate based upon the previously mentioned factors. We do recommend that you start on the higher side rather than lower. First, you never know; someone may grab it at a higher price. Second, like a bottle of wine, a low price conveys low value. Third, you can always reduce the price at any time (and that won't cost you any gas on OpenSea).

Starting an Auction. There are two types of auctions that you can conduct on OpenSea: a regular English auction and a Dutch auction.

English Auction

An *English auction* is a typical auction where bids start low and then increase, with the NFT being awarded to the person who made the highest offer when the auction ends. You'll need to set a minimum starting bid amount, and you'll also need to set a reserve price for the auction, which is a minimum price you're willing to accept for the NFT. If no one made a bid at least as high as the reserve price when the auction ends, the NFT will not be sold.

Note that on OpenSea, if a bid is made within the last 10 minutes of the auction, the remaining time will be increased by 10 minutes. This is to prevent people from sniping an NFT at the last second so that all potential buyers have an opportunity to bid.

Generally, bidding doesn't heat up until near the very end of the auction, as potential buyers don't want to show their hand too early. So, if the auction starts out slow, don't get discouraged.

If the auction ends without a buyer, don't worry. You can always start another auction for the NFT anytime, list the NFT for a set price, or just leave it open for offers.

Dutch Auction

A *Dutch auction* is where the price of the NFT starts out high and then slowly decreases over time. The first person to accept the price wins, so there's not a series of bids like in an English auction. The advantage of a Dutch auction is fear of missing out (FOMO). Participants fear that if they wait too long, someone else will grab the item. And there's no second chance for bidders. Once someone grabs the NFT, the auction is over.

We recommend setting a starting price significantly higher than what you think the NFT may be worth. You never know; someone might grab it early.

On OpenSea, you'll get to choose the starting price, ending price, and duration. OpenSea will automatically lower the price in proportional increments until the end date.

Create a Bundle.   Another way that you can sell your NFTs is in a bundle. A *bundle* is a group of NFTs sold as one package. You can group any NFTs you own together. The advantage of a bundle is where you have a whole set of certain NFTs. For example, people are selling bundles of four Rob Gronkowski NFTs, one of each championship NFT.

Note that when selling a bundle on OpenSea, you can do it only with a set price.

Listing Your NFT for Sale

In this section, we'll walk you through, step-by-step, how to list your NFT for sale. Before following along, we recommend reviewing your collection settings. The way your collection looks and its description are part of how your NFT is presented. Most importantly, check that the ongoing royalty percentage is set how you want it and that your payout address is correct. See Chapter 6, "Creating and Minting NFTs."

On OpenSea, go to the page of the NFT that you would like to sell. Click the **Sell** button in the upper-right corner of the page, and you'll arrive at the listing page (see Figure 7.5).

The first thing that you should do is to check that your ongoing royalty rate is correct. It should appear toward the bottom of the right column, in the **Fees** area, under the percent to OpenSea. If you don't see your collection's name and the rate you set, or the

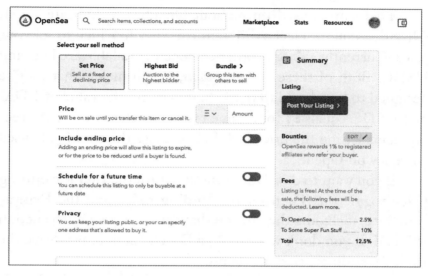

FIGURE 7.5   OpenSea listing page

rate is incorrect, go back and edit your collection settings before proceeding.

Type of Listing.   If your ongoing royalty looks good, the next step is to choose the type of listing. Select **Set Price**, **Highest Bid** (start an English auction), or **Bundle**. If you would like to start a Dutch auction, select **Set Price**.

Set Price
Use Figure 7.5 as a guide. The default currency in which to set your price is ETH, which is indicated by the three horizontal lines icon, as shown in Figure 7.6.

FIGURE 7.6   Ethereum icon

This icon is used throughout OpenSea to indicate ETH. Click the icon to select a different currency in which to set your price. Currently, the only other currencies available are DAI and USDC. Both of these are *stablecoins*, which means that they're designed to be pegged to the U.S. dollar. So, the value of 1 DAI or 1 USDC equals $1 (or a value extremely close to $1). We recommend setting the price in ETH, as that's the commonly used currency on OpenSea.

If you want to do a Dutch auction, turn the **Include ending price** toggle on. Then set the **Ending price** and the **Expiration date**, including the time on that date that the Dutch auction will end. If you don't want to do a Dutch auction, just leave the **Include ending price** toggle off.

If you want your listing to start in the future, turn the **Schedule for a future time** toggle on. Select the date and time at which you would like the listing to start.

If you would like to sell the NFT privately (to a specific person), turn the **Privacy** toggle on. Then enter the buyer's ETH address. The listing will not be public, and only the person connected to the address that you entered will be able to purchase the NFT.

Highest Bid

Select **Highest Bid** to start a regular English auction. Use Figure 7.7 as a guide.

First, you should set the **Minimum bid**. As with **Set Price**, you can select the currency. We recommend setting a low minimum bid, such as `.01 ETH`. You can even leave it at `0` too. If you want to convey a high value, you can set a higher minimum bid, but be aware that it may hamper getting that initial bid.

Next, you need to set a **Reserve price**. A reserve price is required on OpenSea, and it must be at least 1 ETH. As mentioned, if the highest bid at the end of the auction is not at least

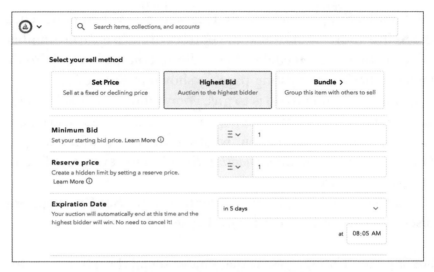

FIGURE 7.7   OpenSea Highest Bid setup

as high as the reserve price, then the auction will end without a sale. So, don't make the reserve price too high.

> *You can accept any bid before or after the auction ends on OpenSea.*

Finally, you'll need to set the **Expiration Date** of the auction, including the time on that date that the auction will end. It's good to give yourself enough time to spread the word about the auction. On the other hand, it's advantageous to create a sense of urgency, which would favor a shorter auction duration. We suggest five days, but three and seven are fine too. Note that you cannot currently set the auction to start at a future date on OpenSea.

Bundle

Select **Bundle** to sell two or more NFTs as a bundle. You will be taken to your account page to select which NFTs to include in the bundle. Simply click an NFT to select it. When done, click the **Sell Bundle of** button at the bottom of the page (the number of NFTs that you selected will be indicated on the button). You'll be taken back to the listing page, as shown in Figure 7.8.

The first thing to do is to give your bundle a name. We suggest having a descriptive name, so potential buyers won't have to guess or be confused about what's in the bundle, for example, *GRONK Super Bowl Championship Bundle*. However, feel free to get creative as well.

The remaining options are identical to the **Set Price** options discussed earlier. Please refer to that section.

Posting Your Listing.   Now that you've set all the parameters for your listing, make sure that everything looks good in the summary area on the right side of the listing page. See Figure 7.5 earlier in this chapter.

If everything looks good, click the **Post Your Listing** button. If this is the first time listing an NFT for your account, your

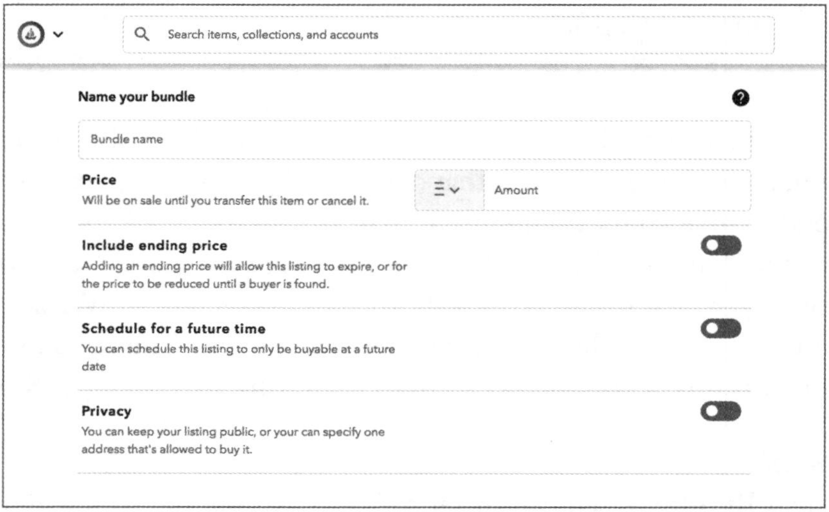

FIGURE 7.8   OpenSea Bundle setup

MetaMask wallet should pop open, showing the required gas fee that you need to pay. If your MetaMask wallet didn't automatically pop open, then open it manually. Note that the total fee is the same as the gas fee.

If gas fees are currently high or your balance is too low to cover the gas fees, you can reject the transaction and try listing the NFT later. If you need to add ETH to your MetaMask wallet, follow the procedures laid out earlier in this chapter.

If everything looks good, click the **Confirm** button in your MetaMask wallet. Your transaction may take a few minutes to be confirmed by the Ethereum network. It may take a little longer if network congestion is high, so please be patient. After the transaction is confirmed, you may also have to confirm a small transaction to approve WETH spending. See Chapter 8 regarding WETH. After that is complete, your NFT should be listed. Congratulations! You've got an NFT for sale.

The next time that you list an NFT (and all future times as well) in your account, you won't have to pay any fees. When you click **Post Your Listing**, your MetaMask wallet will pop open. This time, all you'll have to do is click the **Sign** button. Note that if you create a new OpenSea account, you'll need to pay gas fees for your first listing in the new account.

Now that you've got an NFT for sale, it's time to get some potential buyers interested and excited. For that, we turn to marketing your NFT.

Marketing Your NFTs

One of the biggest fallacies of accomplished businesses, entertainers, and celebrities is the idea of "overnight success." We crave these stories because it makes anything attainable to anyone by the mere stroke of luck. The NFT space is flush with dreams of overnight successes. Because this space is new to many onlookers, perhaps like yourself, it can be easy to look at successful NFT sales as overnight successes. Whether or not they were established artists with an audience prior to their foray into NFTs, we assume that they dropped an NFT, people magically found it, and then decided to spend money on it. We routinely overlook the backend grunt work to find buyers and market the NFT, skipping straight to the end result.

If you create and mint an NFT today, post about it on social media tomorrow, and drop it on a marketplace the following day, you likely won't get a single bite. Why?

First, there's competition. There are more than enough NFTs out there to go around. And if you don't communicate why yours is valuable, people simply won't care. There are alternatives. And just because it makes sense in your mind, if you don't establish a rapport with collectors, then they'll never see this same value.

Second, your existing reputation doesn't automatically translate to an NFT reputation. We have seen countless celebrities with 10 million or more followers who cannot get a single bid on their NFTs. We have seen artists with a strong history of physical art sales transition to the digital landscape and flop. We won't divulge who these examples are, as there's nothing to be gained by dragging them through the mud. Realistically, all we can learn is that selling NFTs is complex and not to be taken lightly, no matter who you are.

Third, there's no NFT algorithm that will promote and grow your NFT collector base. This isn't Twitter or Instagram, where you're always a couple of hashtags and an Explore page or Trending page away from going viral. We've become accustomed to growing algorithmically and creating content that appeals to what the algorithm will deliver to people. But there's no algorithm on any NFT marketplaces. You have to send the buyers to your NFT. Nobody else will do it for you. Even if you convince the curators at OpenSea to put you on the home page, it doesn't guarantee sales. We browse their curated selections all the time and often see the same NFTs for a week on the featured home page with no sales.

This shouldn't scare you, though. "You have to realize that behind the $69 million sales . . . there's very modest prices that are supporting a lot of legitimate artists," NFT artist Matt Kane said in a CNBC interview.

Not every NFT is going to knock it out of the park and command six-figure prices. And your goal shouldn't be to make a couple of NFTs that will instantly provide you with enough money to retire on Easy Street. It's just not likely to happen. However, with the right marketing strategy, you can create a collector base that wants to support your work long-term. You can carve out a slice of this growing market and build a supplemental revenue stream that's meaningful to you.

How? Well, NFT sales are all about community.

Building a Community

Marketing an NFT today is more similar to marketing a podcast than anything else. You can record a podcast and drop it on Spotify and Apple Music, but no one is going to find it unless you have a creative way to promote it. There's no algorithm. You have to build your following. You have to decide who your audience will be and what angle your podcast is going to take. How are you reaching this audience? What are you doing to entice them to listen for the first time? Within the podcast's content, what value are you providing to listeners that will make them want to come back? Finally, are you creating something that your core listeners want to share with their friends, thus giving you an additional growth opportunity?

With regard to NFTs, you need to think about the same questions when building a community of collectors. Your existing fans have followed you for a plethora of other reasons over the years, and you're introducing them to something entirely new in NFTs, which they may or may not care about. Your existing audience may not even be the people who come to collect your NFTs. That's something to think about as well.

We often see podcasts fall trap to the copy-cat philosophy. A podcast gets so good at growing its community of listeners that others copy them nearly identically. Look at what *Serial* did for the True Crime genre of podcasts. It's become the most prominent style of podcast production, creating countless spin-offs with a slight twist.

This applies to NFTs too. Specifically, a complete copying of art aesthetics. There are thousands of NFTs that use the Pokémon card format to encapsulate their artwork. The success of the 8-bit CryptoPunks project spurred an entire revolution of computer-generated 8-bit NFT projects.

It works for some, but ultimately by copying others, you create a ceiling on the size of your community of collectors simply because you'll never surpass the original creator.

In this vein, there's no template or quick hack to follow for building your community of collectors. It's going to be different for everyone. What worked for Qu's NFT won't work for Matt's NFT, and so on and so forth.

The bottom line is that everyone's NFT marketing strategy should revolve around building a community of collectors. This can be 3 people or 3,000 people. But the end goal here is to create superfans of your digitized assets — people who will take pride in saying that they were an early collector of your work. Your NFT collectors might come from you educating and converting your existing fans. They might represent an entirely new audience. By focusing on building your community of collectors, you create a long-term growth strategy that will carry you for years, not for one NFT release.

The tactics and tricks that worked once won't necessarily work again. But the principles behind what you should do are sound.

Know Your Audience. When Blake Jamieson started making art professionally in 2016, he leaned into the connections that he had from his previous career in marketing to determine the direction of his art. In his interview with CNBC, he intelligently relayed what all great marketers know, "Who are you serving, and what problem are you solving?" Having a big backlog of tech clients for whom he provided services as a marketer, there was one thing that stood out to him about these high-growth tech startups: Their offices lacked color. So, his tagline became "I make art for offices." His career took off, creating all types of artwork for office spaces.

As his following grew, he made the sound move of talking with his audience. One of those audience members was former NFL wide receiver Jarred Fayson. Fayson loved Blake's work and knew his style could go far with other athletes. So, Fayson asked Jamieson to create three works free of charge for a few of his athlete friends on the basis that they'd promote his work, and naturally, other athletes would come inbound. Jamieson trusted Fayson and went with his plan, which worked wonderfully. Jamieson began getting DMs from athletes who saw his work in their teammates' lockers. Jamieson changed his tagline to "I make art for athletes" almost immediately thereafter. Ultimately, his work within the athletic space would get him recognized by Topps, the sports cards creator, and Jamieson was employed for the insanely successful Topps Project 2020 — a project that brought artists from all disciplines to reimagine 20 iconic baseball cards in their own style.

That same year, Jamieson began his foray into NFTs. Armed with the knowledge of who his audience is, Jamieson has leaned into the Pop Art meets Athlete Portraits and has had great success thus far selling his NFTs. But this is the case only because he spent time learning about his audience and pivoting to create art that satisfies both himself and what his audience desires.

How do you get to know your audience?

Talk to your fans. Plain and simple. It sounds straightforward because it is. But so many people don't do it. Many of us forget that there are actual people behind the accounts that follow us. And they're there for a reason. Find out why and build from there.

What does your audience expect from you? Why do they follow you? Is it your art they rock with, or is it *you* that they rock with? There's a difference.

Once you know your audience, you can begin the process of education—both educating them on NFT collecting and also why you're getting into NFTs.

Content Marketing and Education. How do you market your Instagram account? Through content, of course. The same applies to NFTs. If the content doesn't resonate with people, you'll never sell an NFT. Sharing your work is where NFT sales start.

There's a great book by Austin Kleon called *Show Your Work!: 10 Ways to Share Your Creativity and Get Discovered* (Workman Publishing Company, 2014), which describes the importance of, you guessed it, showing your work as you're creating it. He outlines 10 principles of getting your work noticed:

1. You don't have to be a genius.
2. Think process, not product.
3. Share something small every day.
4. Open up your cabinet of curiosities.

5. Tell good stories.
6. Teach what you know.
7. Don't turn into human spam.
8. Learn to take a punch.
9. Sell out.
10. Stick around.

The principles apply to artists, designers, web developers, and comedians—you name it. And the same can be said for NFT creators.

If this is your first day studying NFTs, then don't be afraid to showcase the process of you learning about NFTs. Make a video of you researching, asking questions of NFT experts, and learning about NFTs. Hop on FaceTime with an NFT artist and make a video of your discussion. Show the process of creating your NFTs and the thought that's going into why you're making this or that NFT.

You have to warm people up to your eventual NFT drop because NFTs are new to 99 percent of people. Many people make the mistake of waiting until the day before, the day of, or the day after their NFT release to tell their fans about their NFT. Ultimately, they find that many of their fans aren't even prepared to buy an NFT. They don't have a digital wallet. They don't have any cryptocurrency. They don't understand why there's value in buying and collecting digital assets.

You have to create hype and demand for your NFT, and that means showing your work to them in stages. Wherever your audience is (Facebook, Instagram, Twitter, TikTok, an email list, and so on), continue communicating with them there. You don't need to create an entirely new channel for your NFT voyage.

In this process of talking about your foray into NFTs, you might find that there are people in your audience who know about NFTs. They may give you some guidance. They may even tell you what they want to collect from you and become one of your first buyers.

Pplpleasr (pronounced "people pleaser") is an excellent example of an NFT artist who shows her work. Even though she's "made it" as an NFT artist by many people's standards, she continues to update her following on what she's thinking about next. Recently, she put herself out there by publishing criticisms of the centralized nature of NFT marketplaces. It's a courageous move to expose oneself like this, but she's sharing her process of learning. And she's not afraid to ask questions, have theories, and foster discussions.

One of the NFT artists that QuHarrison is collecting avidly is the Kingdom of Assassin's manga, created by Elmer Damaso and Erik Mackenzie. The NFTs they're releasing are nothing more than pictures of the sketches they made for the manga series. Even though the manga comic books have been out for years, Qu is drawn to the ability of owning the work that predated the finals. He's collecting their process of showing their work.

Content marketing your NFT serves many purposes, from educating your audience about NFTs to gauging their interest in owning them to creating new audience members who find you through this content. The more time that you spend sharing and creating content about NFTs, the more time you give yourself to find collectors.

Converse with Collectors.   It's not hard to find NFT collectors. You can go straight to Foundation or OpenSea and find the owner of any NFT. Some of these accounts have their Twitter handle on their profile. It doesn't hurt to reach out to them.

There are people behind these wallets and NFT transactions. Many of them are delighted to talk with newbies in the NFT space and share their insights.

Ask them why they bought certain pieces in their collection. Was it for investment, speculation, the aesthetic of the piece, supporting the artist, to create a revenue stream from owning that artwork, or some other reason that you cannot fathom? Ask them which NFT artists are designing their NFT drops well. Be curious and ask them what you want to know.

Every great marketer talks to their customer. They learn from them and come to know them front to back. Then they design things that appeal to them and provide them value.

Not to get your hopes up, but we've even heard stories from "NFT whales"—accounts known for buying a lot of NFTs—getting a DM from an NFT artist politely asking them to check out their NFTs, which they do and go on to purchase.

You never know what direction these conversations with existing NFT collectors will take. Regardless, they've been in the NFT space longer than you and have a wealth of knowledge to share. Not to mention that they've been convinced in some way or another to spend their money on digital assets. That alone is interest enough around which to start a conversation.

Market Making

The heavy lifting of marketing your NFT is all the work you do finding collectors up until dropping your NFTs. But once you know who your collectors are and have prepared them for your NFTs, now you have to create the market for your NFTs. You have to get your collectors aligned and ready for your drop.

In the stock world, pre-IPO companies go on these trips called *roadshows*. Before their IPO, a company will go around to investment banks and convince them why they're the hottest new stock in the game. The bankers review the financials, set the price, get their pre-IPO deals, and then take it to the public market. Because of this work on market-making, companies now have several bankers who've bought into the company's vision, also acting as marketing vessels on their behalf. They're writing press releases, going on Jim Cramer's *Mad Money*, and just generally spreading the gospel of the stock.

Market-making for NFTs is similar. You need to do your own "IPO roadshow," preparing people for your drop. This means speaking with your interested collectors around pricing, the number of editions, perks they might think would be enticing, and so forth. Ideally, in this process, you get some commitments from your potential collectors to start the bidding on drop day.

Editions, Perks, and Price.   The purpose of market-making is to create demand among many collectors. If there's only one customer for a product, then it's not a market. A market consists of many buyers. Therefore, the number of editions that you release, the price of each edition, and the NFT's perks should all align to maximize the number of collectors in your market.

The number of editions that you drop is your supply. If we think back to rudimentary economics, where your supply and demand meet is the optimal price. Too much supply, and people will think your price is overvalued, and thus demand decreases. Too little supply, and you leave money on the table by not fulfilling demand. We recommend erring on the side of lesser supply, given that you can still collect a royalty on resales. However, this is where your grunt work of finding collectors will come in handy. Do you want everyone who desires your NFTs to have one? Then drop many editions of the same piece. Would you prefer that your NFTs are more exclusive and something to be sought after? Then go lower on the number of editions.

A great example of this is DJ Skee's collaboration with Topps on the Project70 sports cards. He's played around with market-making dynamics by allowing the market demand to determine the supply of each card. He sells each card for only three days. The number of people who buy is how many editions they create. It will be interesting to see how his collectibles fare on the resale market, since you could make the argument that initially lower-demand cards become more exclusive in the long run.

Don't be afraid to experiment with different ways of determining your NFT supply.

Another point to consider when market-making is the perks that you offer to NFT buyers. Physical perks open up the demand for your NFTs to more people, given that you can tie your NFT to a physical experience that may have more value in the eyes of collectors.

Famous hip-hop artist A$AP Rocky dropped seven different NFTs in April 2021. The main attraction of the NFTs was a "1 of 1" NFT containing an unreleased A$AP Rocky song snippet titled *$ANDMAN*. While the unreleased music itself was enticing, he added to the appeal by including an in-person recording studio session with him. This opened up the demand base from just A$AP fans to other musical artists who might want to get in the studio with him, as well as others who might just want to see what it's like for A$AP to make the magic happen. Ultimately, the piece sold for more than $50,000.

What can you provide as perks to add to the initial demand for your NFTs? In the conversations you've had with collectors, what did they say they would love to have or do with you?

From a longevity perspective, it can be a big trap to lean too heavily on the perks to drive the price of your NFT. Whatever you can do to cultivate your community of collectors is advised. However, don't get trapped in the mindset that these physical experiences are the NFT because they're not. These are marketing tactics at their core. And once perks are redeemed, they no longer add value to owning that NFT.

And then we get to the price. The main advice that we can provide is to align your price with your goal. This depends entirely on your collectors and what they're willing to spend. Set it at what you think is fair to them, and don't overthink it. Nobody truly knows what an NFT is worth. It's entirely what someone is willing to pay. Once again, it's usually better to start low and build an avid collectorship than it is to shoot for the moon out of the gate.

This brings us to one of the better market-making tactics out there today: free NFTs.

Free NFTs.   A great way to get people excited about your work is simply to give it away to people for free. It sounds counterintuitive that something you give away for free would ever have value in the future. However, a lot of hit NFT projects today started out free. Whether it's CryptoPunks, which gave away all 10,000 Punks from the start, or Beeple, who made all of his work open in the Creative Commons for more than a decade, they provided value to people first and benefited monetarily later.

Your goal in market-making is to build momentum and interest in your NFTs. The more people who you can get collecting your pieces, the greater their appeal because now they become items to desire.

Jessica Ragzy, for example, is a *LEGO Masters* Finalist. She's a big deal in the world of LEGOs. And she sells her LEGO-inspired NFTs at a meager price to get collectors involved. Every day she drops a new piece that is as low as $50 or so to buy. Could she demand a higher price? Most likely. However, she's building a collector base.

If it cost people $500+ to buy a pack of baseball cards from Topps, the number of collectors out there would be a fraction of what it is today. But for a few dollars, you can get into their universe and start collecting.

There's something to be said about foregoing monetary gain initially, whether through free NFTs or low-priced NFTs, so that everyone can get involved. Not only do you grow your collector base through this process, but you also allow your early collectors to benefit later from resales. And if you can create an NFT that helps someone else make a little money in the future, then they're going to keep coming back for more and will happily tell the world about how great your NFTs are.

Put in the Work

The same way that we started this section on NFT marketing is how we'll close it. There are no overnight successes in NFTs. Show us a successful NFT sale, and we'll tell you about the work they put into marketing their NFT beforehand.

Some people have an easier time marketing and selling their NFTs than others. Some people may have used a marketing process that seems like a formula. But there are no formulas for marketing your NFT—just hard work, lots of sharing, conversing with people, and finding a way to cut through the noise.

8

Buying NFTs

There are millions of non-fungible tokens (NFTs) in the various NFT marketplaces. Say that one or two catch your eye. If the price is right, why not put in a bid or buy it outright?

In this chapter, we'll go through, step-by-step, how to buy NFTs. We'll also offer strategies for building a collection. But first, we'll discuss various reasons to buy NFTs.

Why Buy NFTs?

A common question we hear goes something like this: "Why buy NFTs when you can access and display an NFT's image or video without having to buy it?" At the heart of this question is a common sense argument: "Why pay for something that you can get for free?" But this is really a question concerning the technology that makes NFTs unique and scarce, which we covered in Chapter 1, "What Are NFTs?"

This section does not address the technological reasons for buying an NFT, but rather the underlying personal reasons. There can be quite a few reasons, some of which also pertain to why people buy physical art. Some of these reasons are as follows:

- Meaning
- Utility
- Investment
- Prestige
- Collecting

These reasons are not separate and distinct, and a few may apply to any particular NFT purchase.

Meaning

Like a painting or any other work of art, an NFT can move you emotionally, acting as a lens and uncovering deeper meaning or greater understanding, just like Beeple's Cyberpunk-inspired NFTs resonated with how people view and feel about the current state of the world and where we may be headed.

Perhaps you identify with the artist and what he or she stands for or has gone through. Their story touches you through their NFTs. Or you may be an avid *Back to the Future* fan, and the 3D DeLorean NFT with the flux capacitor is something you just have to have.

Whatever meaning an NFT has for you is reason enough to buy it.

Utility

Several types of NFTs provide utility, such as in-game items, domain names, and virtual real estate. Say that you want to give your car a boost in F1 Delta Time. Try upgrading your transmission for example, with a transmission NFT. Now a transmission NFT may not provide a lot of meaning, but it could offer significant utility.

The purpose of the .eth and .crypto domain names, for example, is to provide utility. You can use them in place of lengthy cryptocurrency addresses. But a blockchain domain name can provide meaning as well, as it's a way to represent yourself, like an alter ego.

Digital real estate, like actual real estate, also has utility and meaning. It's a place where you can build and live, while in a particular location that you enjoy.

Investment

We get asked another question frequently, "Are NFTs a good investment?" We're not offering any financial advice, but we will provide our opinion. If you believe that NFTs are still at an early stage and will be the next big thing, then NFTs would seem to be a good investment in general. But you can't invest in NFTs "in general," only in specific NFTs. So, if you're buying NFTs for investment, what would be some good NFTs in which to invest?

The answer depends upon your investment goals. As in the art world, works of established, well-known artists have demand and are more likely to increase in (or at least retain) value than works of an unknown artist. However, if an unknown artist blows up, the increase in value could be considerable. It boils down to risk versus reward.

Keep in mind that, generally, investment in art and NFTs is risky. With established artists, you're laying out a lot of money, which is where the risk enters the equation. Over time, the artwork or NFT could be worth many times your investment. For example, Beeple's *Crossroads* NFT was purchased in December 2020 for $66,666 and then resold two months later for $6.6 million.

There's obviously no guarantee that an established artist's work will garner a high return. In fact, the value could drop. But for an established artist, the drop would hopefully not be significant. Note that as we covered in Chapter 3, "Why NFTs Have Value," there's the additional risk of physical artwork being discovered as a forgery.

On the other end of the investment equation is speculation. This is where you're buying works of unknown or lesser-known artists, or NFT creators, hoping that the artist takes off with the prices of their works in tow. Since NFTs of lesser-known artists will generally be less expensive, you have the opportunity to diversify your risk among multiple artists. If one of them hits, you could earn a sizeable return, taking into account all of your NFT investments. See the "Building an NFT Collection" section later in this chapter.

Some people like to invest in collectible NFTs. For example, they buy multiple NBA Top Shot packs hoping to land LeBron James or another big star and then sell the high-demand NFT on the secondary marketplace for a nice return. For instance, in April 2021, a LeBron James NBA Top Shot moment NFT of a dunk honoring Kobe Bryant sold for $387,600.

One advantage of investing in NFTs, and art in general, is that you're able to enjoy the NFTs you bought, especially if they have meaning to you.

Prestige

Let's face it, lots of people like to show off, and there's nothing wrong with that. Purchasing and displaying art and NFTs is a great way to do it. Lazy.com is a site built for that purpose. There, you can show off your NFT collection. People can also look up your name or Ethereum address on one of the marketplaces and see your collection there as well.

NFTs are blockchain based, and blockchains were designed to be transparent. So, in a way, NFTs were intended to be shown off.

Collecting

We touched on collecting earlier with respect to art NFTs. But NFT collectibles are booming as well. We talked about it in Chapter 2, "What Are NFTs?" People like to collect. And NFTs are fun and easy (once you're on the blockchain) to collect. From CryptoKitties to NBA Top Shot to Garbage Pail Kids, there are tons of great collectible NFTs. What do you like to collect?

For a deeper dive into collecting NFTs, see the section "Building an NFT Collection" later in this chapter.

Buying NFTs

This section presents a step-by-step guide to buying NFTs. As with the earlier chapters, we're going to continue to use OpenSea as a guide, mainly since you're already set up with an account and have your MetaMask wallet connected.

To buy an NFT, you must first find one that you'd like to purchase.

Finding an NFT to Buy

The first step in finding an NFT to buy is to consider why you're buying an NFT. See the previous section, "Why Buy NFTs?" You may have no particular reason other than to try it, and that's fine. But there's probably some type of NFT that you're leaning toward. If not, there are plenty to browse through until something catches your eye (or your heart).

The OpenSea home page is a good place to start. There you'll find sections for exclusive drops and trending collections, or you can browse by category. The categories currently listed on OpenSea are as follows:

- Art
- Music
- Domain Names
- Virtual Worlds
- Trading Cards
- Collectibles
- Sports
- Utility
- All NFTs

The last category, All NFTs, is, in essence, no category if you'd just like to browse everything. There's also a search bar on the OpenSea home page if you have something in mind.

A word of caution: as we discussed in Chapter 2, "What Are NFTs?" anyone can create an NFT with any name, including fake versions of existing items. Please do your own research, particularly when looking for a specific artist, NFT creator, collection, or NFT, to ensure that the NFT is what it claims to be. Look to see if the NFT is in a verified collection—one that has a blue check mark. See the "Verification" section of Chapter 6, "Creating and Minting NFTs." If there's no blue check mark for the collection, the collection could still be fine; just make sure to do your research.

Once you've found an NFT that you'd like to buy, you need to know how it's listed for sale.

Ways to Buy NFTs

As we covered in Chapter 7, "Selling NFTs," there are three ways in which NFTs can be sold:

- Leave it open for offers.
- Set a price.
- Start an auction.

We'll go through how to buy NFTs for each listing method.

NFTs Left Open for Offers. If the NFT you'd like to buy is left open for offers, you can simply make an offer. But there are some steps you must take first.

1. On the NFT's page on OpenSea, click the **Make Offer** button in the Offers section. The Make an Offer pop-up will appear (see Figure 8.1).

   Currently, you can only make offers in WETH, DAI, and USDC. As discussed in Chapter 7, DAI and USDC are stablecoins designed to be pegged to the U.S. dollar. Notice that you can't use ETH to make an offer. So, what is WETH?

   WETH is Wrapped Ethereum, a token with the same value as Ethereum (ETH). The reason why OpenSea uses

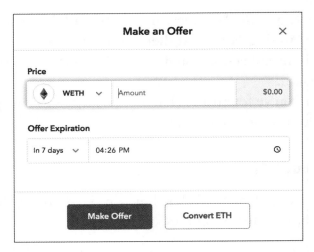

FIGURE 8.1 NFT Make an Offer pop-up on OpenSea

WETH instead of ETH is that WETH has more functionality. For example, if you used ETH for making offers and you wanted to bid 1 ETH on five different NFTs, you would need a total of 5 ETH, one for each NFT. With WETH, if you wanted to bid 1 WETH on five different NFTs, you would need only 1 WETH, not 5. In this case, your WETH would go to the first bid that's accepted, and your four other offers would be automatically canceled unless you have at least 1 WETH left in your wallet to cover them. So, the advantage of WETH is that you can make offers on multiple NFTs with just a small amount.

2. If you don't have any WETH in your wallet, click the **Convert ETH** button in the Make an Offer pop-up. If you do have WETH (or DAI or USDC), skip to step 3.

    In the Convert WETH pop-up, click the **Select a token** button. Then select ETH or another token in your wallet that you would like to convert to WETH.

    Enter the amount of ETH (or another cryptocurrency that you selected) that you'd like to convert to WETH.

We don't recommend converting all your ETH to WETH because you're still going to need some ETH for gas. It's always a good idea to keep some ETH in your wallet because you never know when you may need it for gas. Also, most NFTs on OpenSea with a fixed price are priced in ETH, so if you'd later like to buy an NFT with a fixed price, you should keep some ETH around for that as well.

After you enter the amount to convert to WETH, click the **Wrap** button. Your MetaMask wallet will pop open. If it doesn't, then open your MetaMask wallet. You'll need to pay a gas fee to convert your ETH (or another cryptocurrency that you selected) to WETH. Click the **Confirm** button in your MetaMask wallet. The transaction will likely be pending for a few (or several) minutes. After the transaction completes (is confirmed on the Ethereum network), close out the Convert WETH pop-up.

3. On the NFT's page, click the **Make Offer** button. In the Make an Offer pop-up, enter the amount of WETH that you would like to bid. Obviously, you need to bid more than the current bid. Next, select the Offer Expiration period, which is the time period that you would like your offer to be open and the time of day your offer will expire (on the final day your offer is available). The Offer Expiration period is really up to you. There's no harm in keeping your offer open for a while. Just note that if you'd like to cancel your offer before it expires, then you'll have to pay a gas fee. When ready, click the **Make Offer** button.

Your MetaMask wallet will pop open. If it doesn't, then open your MetaMask wallet. Click the **Sign** button in your MetaMask wallet. There's no fee—you are simply signing.

Your offer should now appear in the Listing section of the NFT's page. You can cancel the offer at any time by clicking the **Cancel** button associated with your offer. Your MetaMask wallet will pop open. If it doesn't, then open your MetaMask wallet. As mentioned, you'll have to pay a gas fee. Click the **Confirm** button in your MetaMask wallet to pay the gas fee and cancel the offer. Or click the **Reject** button if you decide not to pay the gas fee and keep the offer intact.

If the seller accepts your offer, then the sale will be completed. Your WETH (the bid amount) will be sent to the seller, and the NFT will be sent to you. Note that in this situation (on OpenSea), where the seller accepts an offer, the seller will pay gas for the sales transaction.

Congratulations! You are now an NFT collector. You can view your new NFT on your account page. To go there, just click your profile icon in the upper-right corner of any OpenSea page.

NFTs with a Set Price.   If the NFT you'd like to buy has a set price, you can simply accept that price. If you think the price is too high, you can make an offer for less. Just follow the steps in the previous section.

To accept the price, click the **Buy Now** button. On the "Checkout" pop-up, click the **Checkout** button. Your MetaMask wallet will pop open. If it doesn't, then open your MetaMask wallet. You will need to confirm the transaction, which includes a gas fee. Note that on OpenSea, when a buyer accepts a set price, the buyer pays the gas fee. If the transaction looks good, click the **Confirm** button in your MetaMask wallet. Otherwise, click the **Reject** button to cancel the transaction.

You'll be taken to a page saying that your transaction has started and that "The Ethereum network is processing your transaction, which can take a little while." This page may ask for your email address and nickname if you haven't already set that up in your profile settings. Enter an email address and nickname. Note that you cannot have the same nickname as another OpenSea user. Then click the **Save** button. Your MetaMask wallet will pop open. Click the **Sign** button to sign into your OpenSea account.

OpenSea may then send you an email to verify your email address. Click the **Verify My Email** button in the email they sent.

OpenSea will email you when the Ethereum network has confirmed your transaction. Then you will be able to see your new NFT on your account page.

NFTs on Auction.   This section pertains to NFTs being sold by English auction. The previous section also applies to NFTs that are being sold by Dutch auction.

If you'd like to bid on an NFT on auction, click the **Place Bid** button. The "Place a bid" pop-up will appear (see Figure 8.2).

You will only be able to bid in the cryptocurrency with which the NFT is being auctioned (usually WETH). For more information on WETH and how to convert ETH to WETH, see the earlier "NFTs Left Open For Offers" section.

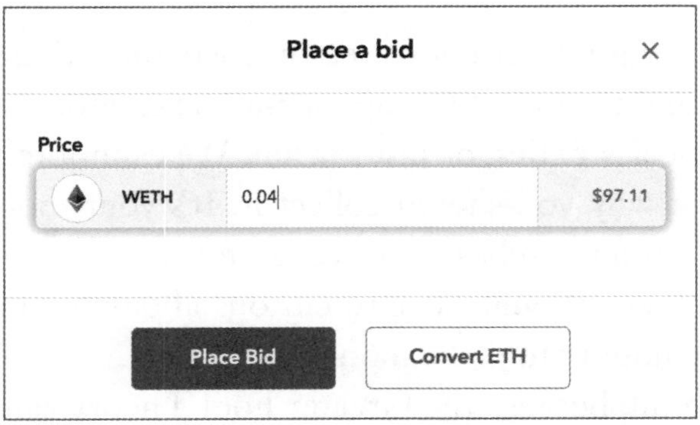

FIGURE 8.2   NFT "Place a bid" pop-up on OpenSea

Your bid amount must be higher than the current highest bid. If you don't have enough funds to make a high enough bid, you must add funds to your MetaMask wallet. See the "Funding Your MetaMask Wallet" section of Chapter 7.

In the "Place a bid" pop-up, enter the amount of cryptocurrency you would like to bid, and then click the **Place Bid** button. Your MetaMask wallet will pop open. If it doesn't, then open your MetaMask wallet. Click **Sign** in your MetaMask wallet to continue with the offer. Note that the buyer of an NFT sold by auction (English auction) will not be responsible for a gas fee.

You will see your offer on the NFT's page in the Offers section. Your offer will be open for seven days. You can cancel your offer at any time, but you will have to pay a gas fee to do so.

If your offer is the highest when the auction ends and your offer is greater than or equal to the reserve price, then OpenSea will automatically complete the transaction. Note that the seller can accept your offer anytime, regardless of when the auction is scheduled to end.

Good luck with your bids.

Building an NFT Collection

We all collect for a variety of reasons, whether it's a childhood passion brought back to life, supporting the creators, the thrill of the hunt, the aesthetics, or just for fun. We cannot tell you what to collect or why you should collect it. It's your money. And if something simply catches your eye, go for it.

Most likely, though, you're curious about NFTs, and perhaps you're hoping to make money with them.

Be careful, because the Greater Fool Theory can be at play in the NFT market. The *Greater Fool Theory* posits that prices go up not due to an increase in value of the item but simply because people are able to sell an overpriced item to a "greater fool." It doesn't matter if the investment is clearly overvalued, so long as there's someone else who will take it off your hands. And, of course, you don't want to be the last person stuck with the investment when there are no greater fools left.

For the vast majority of NFTs, we believe that the Greater Fool Theory will take shape. But that's not to say that all NFTs will fall into this trap. Certain artists will make a name for themselves and become highly sought after for their work, and some NFT projects will create compelling utility and add something to society that is needed.

By no means can we tell you exactly which NFTs those will be. We can, however, outline a few collecting strategies that could put you in a better position for success.

Collect Like an Angel Investor

It can be tempting to put all of your eggs in one basket with NFTs and go all in on just one project—especially when there's a lot of hype and demand around it today. But the danger here is that nobody truly knows who or what will still be around in the near future.

This is why it's wise to invest like an angel investor or venture capital fund. They are known for taking lots of bets on budding businesses. If they're fascinated with app-based insurance, then they find a way to invest in two or three businesses building this future. And even if they cannot get their money in multiple companies building a particular industry in parallel, they still make many investments across several different verticals. Diversification not only gives exposure to lots of different opportunities, but it also reduces risk. It takes only one of those investments to hit it out of the park in order to cover the losses of the other investments—and then some.

It's challenging to pick the NFTs today that will be winners tomorrow. This doesn't mean that there aren't things to look for in a project. Here are some questions to contemplate:

- Who's creating the NFTs?
- Are they putting forth a unique, authentic vision driven by longevity?
- What's the use case or utility of the NFT project?
- Does it seem like a project in which many people will want to partake?
- Is the team responsive to your questions?
- Who else is collecting the project?
- Are there people with extensive collections getting in?
- Has there been any institutional money put behind them?

It's important to recognize and accept that all NFT creators are going to run into challenges. Something happens in life that shifts their attention away from their art. The project could run out of money and stop building additional experiences and NFTs. Their wallet could get hacked, and their NFTs leaked. Copycats could steal some of the demand or, worse, start selling fakes (which happens more than you'd imagine).

Regardless of what happens, you still get a cool piece of art that spoke to you in some way, even if its value plummets. That's why we recommend you collect NFTs that you're entirely OK with never exploding in value. Be an NFT appreciator first and foremost. If you're passionate about the NFTs that you're collecting and you can put into words why you're into a project, others will gravitate to your motives on why you're collecting it.

For this reason, we believe that now is the time to create an identity for what you're collecting.

Have a Collecting Identity

We haven't quite reached the point where people have an ultra-selectivity in how they curate their collections. Most are just money hunting, which is reflected in the mishmash of NFTs in most people's collections.

However, what many people aren't talking about right now is that everyone can create a name for themselves as an NFT collector—not just via headline-grabbing, massive NFT purchases, but rather through how they curate their NFT collection and the identity that they craft around what they collect.

Maybe you collect only movie-based NFTs. Maybe it's NFTs that are the color green. Perhaps you like building a collection entirely consisting of the first NFT that people make. Comedy NFTs, NFTs that support a charity, Pop Art NFTs—there are so many unique features around which you can design your collecting identity.

If we build upon the earlier financial parable, collecting like an angel investor, you can curate your NFT collection in the same way that an *exchange traded fund (ETF)* is built around one particular asset class or theme. ETFs are a type of investment fund that groups assets, such as stocks, bonds, currencies, or commodities, into one asset that you can buy or sell on a stock exchange.

ETFs generally have a theme to the assets they hold. For example, the SPDR S&P 600 Small Cap Growth ETF gives you exposure to 600 companies with high growth potential. The IPAY ETF holds several stocks in the payment processing and digital payments industry, such as Visa, MasterCard, PayPal, and Square.

You can curate your NFT collection in much the same way, building around a theme. Like ETFs, this way of building a collection gives you the diversity of investments that we talked about earlier, while also creating an identity for yourself as a certain type of collector.

Realistically, the only example we've seen of these collector identities would be the Virtual Land Dealers who buy and sell land in blockchain games like *The Sandbox*, *Decentraland*, and *Axie Infinity*. This means that there's ample opportunity to do this in other categories of NFTs.

Designing an identity as a collector is not necessary. However, we feel it's how NFT collecting will evolve over the next decade, especially when you think about the opportunities and streams of revenue that you can build off of this identity. Whether you become a digital gallery curator, build a following in your niche category for breaking out new NFT artists, or some other branding opportunity that we cannot even imagine right now. Not to mention, it would be pretty cool to be able to say you're the longest-living or biggest collector of X, Y, or Z category of NFTs.

Remember, if you buy your first NFT today, then you're one of the first million NFT collectors. That means something. The first million people on Twitter had a lot of opportunities to build a following before everyone else got involved. The first million Instagrammers, when it was primarily a photography sharing app, could break ground and do things no one else was doing. Who knew that Kim Kardashian would ever come along and use Instagram to build a billion-dollar beauty empire?

Being an early NFT collector gives you opportunities that later collectors simply won't have.

For instance, we believe there's a future where having the ability to curate a remarkable collection will be a business in and of itself. A few years from now, NFT collectors who don't want to put the work into researching and deciding on which NFTs to collect will buy people's entire collection as an easy way to get started. Instead of seeking NFTs on the secondary market, they'll simply find someone's collection they like and buy their entire wallet from them—similar to how people buy kids' entire Pokémon, Yu-Gi-Oh, or Magic: The Gathering deck. Mark our words; this will happen with NFTs, especially considering it'll be a social validator to have a wallet with transactions dating back to 2021, 2020, or even earlier.

Not everyone can be one of the NFT whales, like Whale-Shark or Metakoven. But you can make a name for yourself as a collector in different ways. And a great way to dip your toe into the water is through free NFTs.

Where to Start

Browse around on the NFT marketplaces for a few days. See what people are talking about in different NFT communities on the Internet. Find a few that you really like and try reaching out to the creators. Start some conversations and try to get a sense of where they're taking the project. Heck, you can even reach out to collectors and get a sense from them of how they're thinking about collecting.

As we discussed in the "Marketing Your NFTs" section in Chapter 7, "Selling NFTs," it's possible that there are lots of free NFTs out there. There are various methods as to how these free NFTs are transacted. But most often, you cover the gas fee, and they'll send it your way.

How do you find free NFTs? Go to OpenSea, click the Marketplace drop-down at the top of the page, and click All NFTs. Then sort that list using Price Low to High, and *voilà*! You'll see loads of free NFTs out there.

It's a great way to start your collection without dropping thousands of dollars in a couple of hours. And if you wait for opportune times when gas fees are low, you can be on your way to building a nice collection for just a few hundred dollars.

We're very much in the early days of NFTs, which means that there's an opportunity to have a theory on NFT collecting and just do it. Nobody has a crystal ball, which means that there's no wrong way to collect NFTs.

You can just start with one, and see how you like it. NFT collecting doesn't have to be complex. Don't overthink it, and just start collecting!

9

Legal Aspects of NFTs

Now that you're creating, selling, and buying non-fungible tokens (NFTs), it's essential to know how NFTs may be affected from a legal perspective. With any new use of technology, it usually takes a while for regulatory agencies, legislatures, and the courts to catch up to the technology's rapid adoption. In the meantime, we can extrapolate how the law will be applied based upon how similar technologies, and aspects of the new technology, pertain to settled legal doctrine. No specific legal doctrine has yet been set for NFTs, but we can deduce how the law may be applied by looking more generally at how the law is applied to cryptocurrencies, art, and collectibles.

Although Matt Fortnow is a lawyer, nothing in this chapter is intended, nor should it be construed, as legal advice. It's merely an overview of legal aspects affecting NFTs.

Are NFTs Securities?

Back in the ICO (Initial Coin Offering) heyday in 2017, new coins were popping up all over the place. Although some of these coins were founded on solid technology that provided real solutions, many were based on hype and hope, while others were just out-and-out scams. Some speculators looked for a quick 2x return, while others would *hodl* (crypto for "hold"), hoping the coin would go to the moon. And the scam coins were effectively nothing more than pump-and-dump schemes perpetrated by the coin's founders. Too many investors filing complaints raised the ire of the U.S. Securities and Exchange Commission (SEC). But this begged the question: were cryptocurrencies securities? And why does it matter?

It matters because if a particular investment is a security, then the offering of that security must strictly adhere to rules and regulations promulgated by the Securities Act of 1933. Notice the date of the Act. It was enacted after the great stock market crash of 1929 to protect investors from being defrauded by requiring that investments be subject to various registration requirements (or fall within specific exceptions).

Needless to say, these ICOs were not registered in accordance with the Act. That's fine if the cryptocurrency was not a security. So, were they securities?

The Howey Test

To know whether a cryptocurrency is a security, we must first understand what a security is. We're all familiar with stocks and bonds as securities. But securities also include certain kinds of notes and investment contracts.

In 1946, the Supreme Court of the United States heard the case of *SEC v. Howey*, which involved whether a specific lease-back agreement should be considered an investment agreement. If so, that would make it a security and subject to SEC regulations. The defendants in the case sold land in Florida on which there were orange groves. They then offered the purchasers of the land the opportunity to lease back the land to the defendants, who would then manage the groves, produce the fruit, and share the profits with the land purchasers. Not being farmers or knowing how to manage an orange grove, most purchasers took the defendants up on their offer and leased back the land.

The SEC stepped in and sued the defendants, claiming that these transactions constituted investment contracts and thus were securities. The defendants argued that they were merely selling property and then leasing it from the owners.

In its landmark decision, the Supreme Court outlined four factors for determining whether an investment is a security, to become called the Howey test:

1. An investment of money
2. In a common enterprise
3. With the expectation of profit
4. To be derived from the efforts of a promoter or other third party

The Court determined that:

1. The purchasers invested money.
2. There existed a common enterprise of the defendants managing the orange groves on multiple tracts of land.
3. The purchasers had an expectation of profits from the land.
4. The profits were derived from the efforts of the defendants managing the land.

Thus, the Court concluded that the defendant's scheme did constitute a security, stating:

"Thus, all the elements of a profit-seeking business venture are present here. The investors provide the capital and share in the earnings and profits; the promoters manage, control, and operate the enterprise. It follows that the arrangements whereby the investors' interests are made manifest involve investment contracts, regardless of the legal terminology in which such contracts are clothed."

Using the Howey test, the SEC determined that ICOs were indeed securities offerings:

1. The purchasers invested money or cryptocurrency (something of value).
2. A common enterprise existed in that ICOs were generally run by one organization or group of people that created, operated, and promoted the underlying cryptocurrency and ICO.
3. The purchasers had an expectation of profits from their investment in the ICO.
4. The profits were derived from the efforts of the organization or group of people running the common enterprise.

This meant that ICOs would be required to adhere to the SEC filing regulations or utilize an exception such as Regulation D, which has its own set of requirements. The SEC cracked down on specific fraudulent ICOs, declared Bitcoin and Ethereum not securities, and suggested that all other cryptocurrencies were likely securities. This specter created a major damper on ICOs and the whole cryptocurrency market, driving ICOs overseas, in which U.S. investors could not participate. Unable to sustain the mania, the cryptocurrency market crashed in 2018 and lay dormant for a few years.

So, Are NFTs Securities?

Being that the SEC deemed that ICOs are securities offerings and that most cryptocurrencies may be securities, one might presume that NFTs, also being cryptocurrencies (with a supply of 1), are likely to be deemed securities as well. But most feel that NFTs are probably not securities. However, the SEC has not issued any guidance on NFTs yet, so one must still be aware of the possibility that it may land on the side of NFTs being securities.

Let's utilize the Howey test:

1. Purchasers of NFTs invest money or cryptocurrency (something of value).

2. There generally do not seem to be common enterprises associated with NFTs. Instead, most NFTs are one-offs or limited editions of digital art, are collectibles, or have some utility, such as an in-game item.

3. Some people may purchase NFTs as an investment, with an expectation of profit, while others purchase NFTs for their subject matter and for building a collection.

4. Generally, there's no third party promoting the value of NFTs that have been sold.

There's no definitive answer, but NFTs (being non-fungible) are more akin to works of art or collectibles, which are not securities, than to fungible cryptocurrencies. If an NFT has a massive supply or a vast number of editions, it leans more toward a fungible token, and the line becomes less clear.

It's not just the seller of such NFTs who needs to be concerned with it being deemed a security; the exchanges must be concerned as well. If exchanges are providing markets for securities, they must register with the SEC and comply with SEC regulations.

Fractional NFTs

The line becomes less clear, and could even lean toward securities for certain fractional NFTs. *Fractional NFTs* are tokens that represent a fractional ownership of an NFT. For example, the Unicly CryptoPunks Collection (UPUNK) token represents a fractional ownership in a collection of 50 CryptoPunk NFTs. There are 250,000,000 UPUNK tokens in circulation with a market cap (as of this writing) of nearly $30 million.

The UPUNK tokens are similar to cryptocurrencies, fungible with a large supply and an obvious means of investing in valuable NFTs. Also, when it comes to fractionalized art ownership (of traditional physical art), while companies have different business models, most file with the SEC. Accordingly, we feel it's likely that certain fractional NFTs may be considered securities.

Intellectual Property Rights

Intellectual property rights play a significant role with NFTs and art in general. *Intellectual property* is property that derives from creativity. It's a type of property that does not exist in physical form. Intellectual property encompasses copyright, trademark, patent, and trade secrets. For the purposes of NFTs, we're going to focus on copyright and trademark.

Copyright

A *copyright* is, in essence, the right to make copies. According to Dictionary.com, a copyright is "the exclusive legal right, given to an originator or an assignee [transferee] to print, publish, perform, film, or record literary, artistic, or musical material, and to authorize others to do the same."

A copyright is created once the work is fixed in a tangible medium. This means that the work must be on a canvas, written down, recorded, saved onto a disk or drive, or any other kind of tangible medium. In other words, the work can't just be in your head, spoken, sung, or performed, unless the latter three were recorded. A creator does not need to register a work with the U.S. Copyright Office to obtain a copyright, although registration does confer certain advantages.

The copyright is separate and distinct from the actual work. The actual work is the physical artwork, such as a painting, digital work, JPEG image, video, or song. The copyright is the intangible right pertaining to the work that is endowed upon the creator of the work.

When Buying NFTs.   When you purchase an NFT (or any other work of art), you are *not* purchasing the copyright in that NFT. The creator (or artist) retains the copyright. You have the right to use and display the NFT (the copy of the artwork that you have) for personal, and not commercial, purposes. You do not have the right to distribute or sell copies of the NFT's content. Also, you do not have the right to make derivative works (other works based on the NFT's content). Of course, you do have the right to sell the NFT at any time.

Note that you can purchase the copyright in a work, but only if there's an express written agreement assigning the copyright from the creator (or current copyright owner) to you.

Bottom line: Be careful what you do with the NFTs you buy or receive and their content, so that you're not violating the creators' copyrights.

When Creating NFTs.   If you're making an NFT, it's always best to create an original work of art or original design. You cannot use any old image, video, or audio recording that you find on the Internet. Every photo, piece of artwork, and other images, videos, and sound recordings on the Internet (and elsewhere) are protected by copyright. If you use a work that you did not create, then you may (and likely will) be violating the image creator's copyright. In such a case, you may be liable for monetary damages and will likely have to take the offending NFTs off the market.

If there's an existing work that you would like to use, you may be able to get a license from the copyright owner. A license will grant you certain rights to use the copyright in an NFT. In return, you would pay the licensor (copyright owner) a royalty (percentage of sales). The licensor may also request an advance (an up-front payment). Licenses are generally valid for a specified time period in a defined territory. For NFTs, a license should be valid in perpetuity throughout the world.

Certain websites offer royalty-free licenses for images and videos, so you would be able to use those works for free. However, make sure to read the license terms because there may be some restrictions or requirements. For example, you may be restricted from using the work for commercial purposes, or you may be required to attribute the work to the website (write in your NFT's description where the work came from).

You are free to use images or videos (or any other type of work) that are in the public domain. Copyrights last only a limited period of time. For works published in 1978 and later, the duration of copyright in the United States is generally the life of the author plus 70 years. However, for works published before 1978, the duration of copyright in the United States is generally 95 years. So, if a work is more than 95 years old, it's likely in the public domain. Refer to the Resources page of the website (TheNFThandbook.com/Resources) for royalty-free and public domain websites. Note that different countries have different copyright laws and different copyright durations.

Maybe you would like to hire someone to create the artwork or design that you have in mind. If you do, make sure to have a written agreement that expressly states that the work they are creating is a *work made for hire* or *work for hire*. This is a specific legal term that confers copyright ownership upon the party hiring the artist. The other way that a work may be considered a work for hire is if it's prepared by an employee within the scope of his or her employment. The latter would apply only if you're an employer, and it's part of your employee's job to create works of art or designs.

Copyrights as NFTs. Copyrights can potentially be the main content of an NFT. For example, music artists Taylor Bennet and Big Zuu have apparently sold NFTs comprising 1 percent of the sound recording copyright for particular songs. However, upon closer inspection, the purchasers do not own 1 percent of the copyright, but rather a perpetual license to receive 1 percent of the digital royalties earned by a particular song designated in the NFT's description. It may seem like we're splitting hairs, but there's a big difference between owning a copyright and owning a portion of an income stream.

If you owned 1 percent of the copyright, you would be entitled to 1 percent of *all* income earned from the sound recording, not just 1 percent of the digital royalties. So, for example, if the sound recording were licensed for use in a movie or TV commercial for $50,000, an owner of 1 percent of the copyright would receive $500, while an owner of a license to receive 1 percent of the digital royalties would receive nothing from this use.

So, if you're going to invest in a "copyright" NFT, make sure that you know exactly what you're getting. Read the fine print. And if you don't understand it, ask a lawyer.

Each "copyright" NFT by Taylor Bennet and Big Zuu sold for 100 USD Coin (USDC), a value of $100. This type of NFT, a participation in an income stream, seems like an investment, and might be considered a security by the SEC.

Trademark

A *trademark* is generally a symbol, design, word, or phrase (or combination thereof) that identifies the source of goods (products). We're all familiar with the trademarks of Coca-Cola, Apple, Nike, McDonald's, and many others. When you see a phone or laptop with the Apple logo on it, you know that Apple created it, which you also mentally associate with a certain level of quality, reliability, coolness, and a host of other attributes. That's why companies invest lots of money in how their products are perceived.

A *service mark* is similar to a trademark, but it identifies a service, not a product. For example, "Fly the Friendly Skies" is a service mark of United Airlines, a transportation service. Generally, "trademark" is a broad term that encompasses both trademarks and service marks.

If you see the ® symbol next to a company's name, logo, or slogan, it means that the trademark has been registered with the

U.S. Patent and Trademark Office. Registration provides trademark protection throughout the United States. If you see "TM" or "SM" (for a service mark) next to a company's name, logo, or slogan, it generally means that the trademark has not been registered yet. The use of ®, "SM," or "TM" is not required, so if a logo, name, or slogan doesn't have any such designation, it does not mean you are free to use it.

The main crux of trademark law is preventing consumer confusion regarding the origin of goods. Trademark owners are also concerned about potential dilution of their mark, which is when the public's perception of the mark's uniqueness is reduced.

For example, in 2017 In-N-Out Burger sued In-N-Out Cleaners, claiming that the latter's name and logo was confusingly similar to, and diluted, their trademark (see Figure 9.1). In other words, In-N-Out Burger was concerned that consumers would think they were somehow involved in In-N-Out cleaners, and also that In-N-Out Cleaners' logo reduced the uniqueness of In-N-Out Burger's logo.

Both logos contain the same name (In-N-Out) and colors, nearly identical typefaces, and similar placement and angle of the design element (the arrow and the hanger). Although the companies provide distinctly different goods—burgers versus dry cleaning—it seems likely that consumers would be confused as to whether In-N-Out Burger was associated with In-N-Out Cleaners. It also seems that the uniqueness of In-N-Out Burger's logo would be reduced as well.

FIGURE 9.1 Logos of In-N-Out Cleaners and In-N-Out Burger

When it comes to creating NFTs, and artwork in general, it's generally OK to use a company's trademark for commentary, criticism, and parody purposes. The main concept to keep in mind is whether consumers or viewers of your NFT would think that the trademark owner created or endorsed your NFT or its content. Note that the criticism or parody must be aimed at the trademark, not at an unrelated party or issue.

Also, be careful about using a trademarked name or phrase as part of your NFT's name, username, or collection name on an NFT marketplace.

One artist intentionally created an NFT with the logos of every Fortune 100 company. See Figure 9.2.

This NFT seems like a commentary on society, and it would not likely cause viewers to believe that the piece was created or endorsed by any or all of the companies presented, although you never know.

Unfortunately, there's no bright line test to determine whether your use of a trademark is appropriate. Again, we suggest consulting with an attorney.

FIGURE 9.2   "®" NFT

Right of Publicity

The *right of publicity* is the right of individuals to control and profit from their identity (or persona), which includes their name, image, likeness, voice, and other unique identifiers. An obvious example would be that you can't sell T-shirts with Kevin Hart's face on them without his permission. But what about a TV commercial that featured a robot in a blonde wig, gown, and jewelry that turned letters on a set similar to *Wheel of Fortune*? In 1993, the Ninth Circuit Court of Appeals (one step below the U.S. Supreme Court) took the right of publicity to the extreme, holding that the commercial had violated Vanna White's right of publicity, even though the commercial did not contain her image, likeness, name, or voice.

What does this all mean? Generally, you can't use an image or video of someone else in an NFT without their permission . . . but it's not black and white. The previous examples were uses of celebrities' identities for commercial purposes. Artists and NFT creators have a First Amendment right of free speech (at least in the United States), which conflicts with a person's right of publicity, creating a gray area. Are you creating art, or is the use of the person's likeness for commercial purposes?

Let's say that you want to make an NFT of a celebrity such as Snoop Dogg. If you don't intend to sell your NFT or otherwise use it for commercial purposes, you should be fine without his permission. However, if you want to sell it, that could be considered "for commercial purposes," and you might need Snoop's permission. If you made an edition of 100 NFTs of Snoop Dogg, that would weigh in the direction of it being "for commercial purposes," more likely requiring Snoop's permission. So, how can you be more certain whether you're violating a person's publicity rights?

The Transformative Use Test

Gary Saderup is an artist who created a charcoal drawing of The Three Stooges. He then sold lithographs and T-shirts containing the drawing. Comedy III Productions, Inc. owned the publicity rights of The Three Stooges and sued Gary Saderup and his company for misappropriation of the Stooges' publicity rights. The case went all the way up to the California Supreme Court.

The court adopted a *transformative use test*. They asked, "whether a product containing a celebrity's likeness is so transformed that it has become primarily the defendant's own [artistic] expression rather than the celebrity's likeness." The court also expressed that "Another way of stating the inquiry is whether the celebrity likeness is one of the 'raw materials' from which an original work is synthesized, or whether the depiction or imitation of the celebrity is the very sum and substance of the work in question." So, in essence, is the drawing in question more of a work of art or more of just an imitation of The Three Stooges? Although the drawing was an artistic rendering of The Three Stooges, the court determined that it was not transformative enough. In other words, people were buying the shirts mainly because they had The Three Stooges on them, not because they were works of art.

So, when creating NFTs containing a celebrity's likeness (or anyone's for that matter), make it a work of art, not just an imitation of the celebrity.

Getting back to Snoop Dogg, there are actually multiple NFTs on OpenSea (the largest NFT marketplace) that contain his likeness. For example, there's the aptly titled "Snoop Dogg #2," the main image of which is pictured in Figure 9.3. Scrazyone1, the creator of this NFT, is obviously not shy about using Snoop Dogg's name either.

FIGURE 9.3   Main image of "Snoop Dogg #2" on OpenSea

Does this NFT featuring Snoop Dogg pass the "transformative use test?" We won't know unless Snoop sues and it goes to court. But for all practical purposes, Snoop (or any other celebrity) probably won't bring a lawsuit unless you're making significant money with his likeness. More likely, you'd get a cease-and-desist letter. But again, this is not legal advice. We suggest that you consult with an attorney if you plan to use someone's likeness in an NFT.

Licensing Publicity Rights

If you'd like to use the name and likeness of a celebrity, you could make the official NFTs of that celebrity by licensing their publicity rights. A *license* is a contract in which the owner of the rights (the licensor) grants you (the licensee) a limited right to use the name and likeness (and possibly other identifiers) of the celebrity.

Some of the main points of such a license would include the following, among others:

Property: The celebrity (or a movie or comic book character, for example).

Licensed Subject Matter: Name, likeness, voice, trademarks, and so on.

Articles: The items to be manufactured or created and sold, in this case, NFTs.

Territory: The geographic area to which the license is limited. In the case of NFTs, it would be the world, as they're sold worldwide on the Internet.

Term: How long the license lasts.

Exclusivity: Whether or not the licensor can license the rights to someone else during the Term in the Territory.

Royalty Rate: The percent of sales the licensor gets.

Advance: An up-front sum (if any) payable to the licensor.

Guarantee: The minimum amount of royalties (if any) the licensee will owe the licensor regardless of whether there were enough sales to cover it.

As you can surmise, a license of this nature can be quite complex. So, if you do go this route, we highly recommend that you consult with an attorney.

Posthumous Publicity Rights

Is it OK to use the name and likeness of someone who's dead? It depends. While copyright laws are federal laws, publicity rights are left to the states. So, in some U.S. states, dead people (or rather, the deceased person's estate) don't have any publicity rights. In other states, dead people have publicity rights, which the deceased person's estate can enforce. The determinative factor is where the person was domiciled when they died. If it was in a state that doesn't have posthumous publicity rights, then you can generally use that person's name and likeness.

When Marilyn Monroe died of a drug overdose in 1962, she had residences in both New York and California. Although she was living and working as an actress in California at the time, and was seemingly domiciled in California, her estate argued that she was domiciled in New York. They did this to save on estate taxes, which were significantly higher in California. It seemed like a good idea, right?

Fast-forward 50 years. The Marilyn Monroe estate sued various photo libraries that were selling photos of Marilyn Monroe, claiming it violated her posthumous publicity rights, which are protected by California law. One case went up to the Ninth Circuit Court of Appeals, which determined that since Marilyn Monroe's estate had argued decades earlier that she was domiciled in New York at the time of her death, then New York law should apply. Unfortunately for the estate, New York (until last year) did not provide posthumous publicity rights, and thus the defendants were free to use Marilyn Monroe's image. Since this 2012 case, people have been freely using Marilyn Monroe's image on all types of products. For example, see the Marilyn Monroeji app, pictured in Figure 9.4.

So, what seemed like a good decision to save taxes after death turned out to be disastrous for the estate. In 2012 Forbes estimated that the estate's royalties from Marilyn Monroe's publicity rights were $27 million a year, putting her third on the list behind Michael Jackson and Elvis Presley.

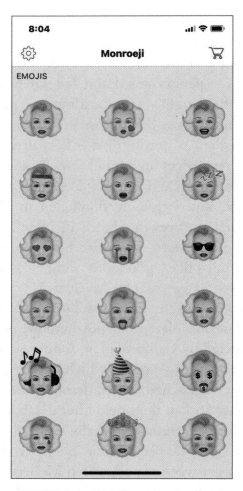

FIGURE 9.4 Marilyn Monroeji app

The lesson here is if you want to use the name or likeness of a dead person, find out where they were domiciled when they died and whether that state's law provides posthumous publicity rights. Note that some states have not formally addressed the issue. Bottom line: We recommend consulting with an attorney.

Keep in mind that just because you might be able to use the name and likeness of a particular dead person, you must still be wary of using an image or video of that person because that particular image (art or photo) or video is most likely protected by copyright. See the previous section on copyright.

Newsworthiness

One caveat to the right of publicity is *newsworthiness*. The First Amendment protects the reporting of newsworthy people or events. Accordingly, courts have generally held that using a person's name or likeness in the news or a literary work, movie, or other entertainment story concerning something newsworthy does not violate that person's right of publicity. However, with respect to NFTs, it seems that this caveat would generally not apply because NFTs are generally not considered a medium for reporting the news.

Right of Privacy

Often, people use "right of publicity" and "right of privacy" interchangeably. However, that would be incorrect because these rights are distinct. The *right of privacy* encompasses a person's rights to the following:

- To not have personal, private information made public
- To be left alone
- To be free from unwarranted government intrusion into our personal lives

With respect to NFTs (and artwork in general), we're concerned about the first aspect, revealing a person's private information. Private information can comprise details of a person's personal life that are not generally known. So, if you're aware of a person's private information, do not include it in an NFT. We like to go by the motto "When in doubt, leave it out."

Public Figures

A caveat to the right of privacy is public figures (celebrities, professional athletes, politicians, and the like). In the United States, because of freedom of speech and the belief that the public has a right to know matters of public concern (further based upon the assumption that everything a public figure does is a matter of public concern), public figures have much weakened privacy rights, similar to the newsworthiness caveat discussed in the previous section regarding publicity rights.

So, with respect to privacy rights, there's less concern if the subject of your NFT is a public figure. However, note that this caveat affects a public figure's privacy rights, *not* their publicity rights. You must still fully respect (or license) a public figure's publicity rights, as discussed in the previous section.

Contracts

Contract law comes into play when the NFT seller offers perks or includes unlockable content in the NFT.

A *contract* is a binding agreement between two or more parties. For a contract to be created, there must be three elements:

- An offer
- Acceptance of the offer
- Consideration, which is what's being provided to, or undertaken by, each party

Let's use the sale of an NFT as an example. Let's say that you list an NFT on a marketplace with the price of 1 ETH. This is an offer; you are offering the NFT for sale. Someone then purchases the NFT. They do this by accepting the offer of 1 ETH. Via the marketplace, both parties provide the consideration. You provide the NFT, and the purchaser provides the 1 ETH in exchange. Another example would be where you have an NFT on a marketplace and someone offers 1 ETH for it. You accept the offer, and the exchange is made. Both of these examples are pretty straightforward.

Perks

If you're offering perks with your NFT, those perks become part of the consideration. The purchaser is making a bid or accepting the price you offer based in part on the perks, and the seller is contractually obligated to deliver the perks as specified (in the description of the NFT). Also, the perks should be delivered or provided in a reasonable, timely manner.

It's vitally important to describe the perks with specificity so that there's no misunderstanding as to what must be delivered. It may help to include detailed terms and conditions in the NFT's description.

The website for Rob Gronkowski's NFTs (GronkNFT.com) has extensive "TERMS & CONDITIONS OF SERVICE FOR NFTS BOUGHT AS PART OF THE ROB GRONKOWSKI CHAMPIONSHIP SERIES NFT AUCTION," which cover several areas, including dispute resolution, in the finest of legalese. These terms begin with this statement:

> "These Terms and Conditions of Service ("T&Cs") constitute a legally binding agreement (the "Agreement") between you (also referred to herein as "User") and Medium Rare Mgmt, LLC ("MRM") governing your purchase of NFTs as part of the Rob Gronkowski Championship Series NFT Auction."

The problem that Gronk's (or Medium Rare Mgmt, LLC's) lawyers may have overlooked is that these terms are not referenced in the NFTs or in the description of the collection. So, how can someone be subject to terms of which they were not made aware?

If you have a dispute concerning the purchase of an NFT, we suggest reaching out to the marketplace (on which the NFT was purchased) for support, although there might not be much they can do. So, particularly when it comes to perks, it's "caveat emptor" (buyer beware) when purchasing NFTs.

NFT Content

As we discussed in Chapter 3, "Why NFTs Have Value," an NFT's main content and unlockable content are not stored on the blockchain. Therefore, it's possible that the location where the content is stored might not be continuously maintained, which could lead to loss of the content, resulting in complete loss of value of the NFT. This is of primary concern for unlockable content, which is more likely to be stored on a personal server or via the creator's personal account on a cloud storage service.

The question arises as to whether the NFT creator is contractually obligated to maintain the NFT's content in perpetuity (forever). Perpetuity is a long time, but one of the main draws of NFTs is their permanence. Since NFTs are blockchain assets, people assume that their existence will be permanent, which would lead to an expectation that the NFT remain permanent. And this expectation would seem to include the NFT's content, both the main content and unlockable content.

Thus, it appears that you should be obligated to maintain an NFT's content in perpetuity. However, in some U.S. states and other jurisdictions, perpetual contracts are unenforceable or terminable as a matter of public policy. It will be interesting to see how courts rule on these competing interests.

Taxes

Unfortunately, NFTs are not immune from taxes. This section explores different areas where taxes may apply to NFTs. It's an overview of the potential tax issues pertaining to NFTs and should not be considered tax or legal advice. We highly recommend that you consult an accountant or lawyer concerning tax issues.

Sales Tax

Generally, sales taxes are applied to the sale of goods and services by the U.S. state (and sometimes local) government in which the sale occurred. With the sale of NFTs, the first question would be, where did the sale occur? Which state's (or other jurisdiction's) sales tax should apply? If goods are shipped out of state, then usually no sales tax is applied, but instead, a use tax may apply in the purchaser's state.

Some states don't charge sales tax on digital items. Are NFTs digital items? Apparently, but some states define digital items as items that were downloaded. Since NFT's are not downloaded (they remain on the blockchain), they might not fall within the digital items' exception in these states.

What if sales tax doesn't apply to digital items, but the NFT contains perks that are physical items or services? Sales tax, in this case, might be applied to the value of the perks. But how should the value of the perks be determined?

Just like Amazon started charging sales tax nationwide in 2017, we wouldn't be surprised if at some point NFT marketplaces unfortunately started charging sales tax on every NFT sale.

Income Tax

If you're creating and selling NFTs, you'll be responsible for paying taxes on your income from those sales. However, you should be able to deduct the expenses that you incurred in connection with your creation, minting, listing, and promotion of your NFTs.

It may be advantageous to form a business and run the NFT sales through that business. We suggest talking to an accountant. Note that there are other potential advantages to forming a business, such as the limited liability a corporation or LLC (limited liability company) provides.

Capital Gains Tax

Generally, if you have an asset that you sell, you will have to pay tax on the gains, the difference between the price you paid for the asset and the price at which you sold it. Like income tax, capital gains tax is charged both at the federal and state levels.

It appears that NFTs are subject to capital gains tax. For example, if you bought an NFT for 1 ETH and sold it for 3 ETH, you would have 2 ETH of gains. However, the IRS is concerned about the value in dollars, not in ETH. Therefore, the gain in value of the NFT would be the dollar value of the NFT when you sold it (the value of 3 ETH at the time you sold the NFT) minus the dollar value of the NFT when you bought it (the value of 1 ETH at the time you purchased the NFT). Again, please consult an accountant.

Note that capital gains tax is owed only when you sell the asset. Once you sell the asset, the capital gains are "realized." Before you sell the asset, any gain in value is considered "unrealized."

Long Term vs. Short Term.   If you sell an NFT that you held for less than one year, that would be considered short-term capital gains, and the tax you owe would be based on your regular income tax rate for both federal and state taxes.

If you sell an NFT that you held for at least one year, that would be considered long-term capital gains, and the federal tax you owe would be based on the capital gains tax rate, which is generally more advantageous than your regular income rate. Although the current rate varies from 0 to 20 percent for stocks and similar investments, NFTs will likely be considered collectibles, which currently have a capital gains tax rate of 28 percent. However, one may argue that certain types of NFTs, such as digital real estate and domain names, are not collectibles.

Note that most U.S. states do not distinguish between long- and short-term capital gains, which are taxed at your regular state income tax rate. However, some states do provide favorable tax treatment for long-term capital gains.

When Buying NFTs.   You may be subject to capital gains tax when buying NFTs if you purchased the NFT with cryptocurrency. For example, if you bought 1 ETH a while back for $1,800 and then later purchased an NFT for 1 ETH when the value of 1 ETH was $3,800, you may owe capital gains tax on the ETH, which increased in value by $2,000. This is because you realized the gain on the ETH when you used it to purchase the NFT. If you bought the NFT more than one year after you bought the ETH, the long-term capital gains tax rate would apply.

The NFT you purchased now has a cost basis of $3,800. So, if you later sell the NFT for a value of $5,000, you will have $1,200 of realized gains on the NFT, for which you will owe capital gains tax.

Overall, keep taxes in mind when buying and selling NFTs, because you don't want to have any surprises later from the IRS or your state or local tax authorities. And, of course, consult an accountant or lawyer regarding tax matters.

10

The Future of NFTs

Non-fungible tokens (NFTs) have a bright future, not just because digital art is a massively underappreciated asset class poised to dominate the art market (although we think this is true); rather, NFTs have a bright future because they're providing a bridge to digital economies that will touch everyone in the future (and even in some cases, today).

Looking at NFTs solely as a speculative art asset is narrow-minded and misses the multitude of future uses of NFTs. We're soon likely to see the NFT-ification of everything from NBA season tickets to rare Mercedes Benzes.

With that being said, there are three distinct areas within the future of NFTs on which you should focus your attention:

- The metaverse
- Nonbankable assets
- Digital wallets

In this chapter, we'll explore each area in detail, showing you the role of NFTs in these multitrillion-dollar futures.

The Metaverse

The Internet has evolved to the point where we can share and communicate almost anything that we want across space and time. We find love through apps. We trust our digital neighbors to give us the best suggestions for food and housing. We place our most precious photographic memories in the hands of digital giants to protect for eternity.

The Internet has become this expansive, virtual, shared space for almost anything you can imagine. We rely heavily on others who share this space to keep us informed, write funny tweets, make interesting content, and much more. But this isn't the best version of the Internet. Like any form of existence, it must continue to grow and evolve.

So, what's next?

The evolution of the Internet is the *metaverse*—a culmination of the shared Internet and the boundless possibilities in augmented and virtual reality technologies. The Internet has done a lot of the grunt work in bringing information, services, and experiences online. But there are more efficient ways to deliver, discover, and interact with everyone and everything that exists on the Internet.

Types of Metaverses

The most common comparable for the metaverse is The Oasis in the movie *Ready Player One*. The Oasis is an online world accessible through virtual reality headsets. Kids go to school in The

Oasis. Entrepreneurs build businesses in The Oasis. Generally speaking, everything takes place in The Oasis.

In reality, we may not reach this level of the metaverse for decades, if ever. Online games like *Second Life* have built toward this, allowing users to host concerts, connect with friends, and create revenue streams in their "second life." But the idea of a one-stop shop for the metaverse is entirely ambitious.

Instead, the metaverse is being built in many different siloes.

Video Game Metaverses.   Video games are probably the closest real-world comparable we have to a thriving metaverse with its own economies. Many of the following games allow players to exist in a fictional world and express themselves in competitive and original ways.

NBA 2K21 gives players a lot of freedom to interact with other players and explore The City—a virtual world with outdoor courts, casinos, training gyms, parks, and lots more. For an avatar to walk from one end of The City to the other would take upward of 45 minutes. So, it's a rather large virtual world.

Fortnite is remarkable, not just because more than 350 million people have played the game, but it's also proven to be flush with ancillary opportunities. Travis Scott and Marshmello have both held virtual concerts in the game. Samsung created a Galaxy skin for Fortnite avatars to promote their Samsung Galaxy Note 9. (Even Louis Vuitton designed an avatar skin for *League of Legends*.)

There are loads of metaverses being built in the form of video games—*League of Legends*, *Minecraft*, *Grand Theft Auto Online*, *Red Dead Online*—the list goes on. Many of these video game metaverses even have their own currency with which to transact different in-game items.

Video games are further along than anyone when it comes to building metaverses. Still, they're not entirely free-form in what you can do. Within the lines of the game, they give players a lot of freedom to roam and express themselves.

Livestream Metaverses.   Aside from the virtual world aspect of metaverses, another equally important quality is the community. Are people engaging in this virtual space simultaneously and concurrently?

Behind the *Super Bowl* and award shows like *The Grammys*, streamers on Twitch, YouTube, Clubhouse, and Discord are some of the most well-versed individuals and groups at getting people to tune in live. Kitboga, for example, streams to hundreds of thousands of people on Twitch while he pranks scam callers. Thousands of people tune in live to "NYU Girls Roasting Tech Guys" on Clubhouse. These are metaverses! Live streamers show how possible it is for people to spend time together voluntarily in an online world around some shared interest.

Sometimes these streamers build up their following by tapping into a shared interest and ask the community to participate. At other times, people tune in just to see the streamer. Regardless, simultaneous experiences are a fundamental part of the metaverse.

Live streaming is missing the immersive component that we see with video games and VR. But these live streamers are just a VR app away from building an immersive metaverse. So, in this sense, they've built great foundations for an immersive metaverse in the future.

VR Metaverses.   Naturally, we cannot talk about the metaverse and not cover what's happening in VR. There are many VR apps built around this idea of a new social experience. AltspaceVR, for example, allows friends and strangers to hang out at live shows, meetups, and classes. OrbusVR provides a unique social VR experience where you can explore the virtual world of Patraeyl, level up your character (as a bard, mage, paladin, shaman, scoundrel, and so on), and connect with other players.

For the time being, most VR metaverses lack scale. There aren't enough people in them concurrently to be engaging long-term. And this is only because VR headsets are not yet ubiquitous like smartphones and laptops.

Regardless, as you can see, we have all of the pieces of a metaverse. But bringing them together in one is a challenge. So, for the time being, metaverses will exist in siloes. However, that doesn't mean that each of these won't grow economically and provide more extensive opportunities for participants.

NFTs in the Metaverse

The more time that you spend in an environment, the more likely you are to come around to purchasing something there. Many people in the Chicagoland area scoff at a $10 Miller Lite, but when you're at a Cubs game, you're bound to cave and buy one. This sentiment is even more true for environments you choose to be in—video games especially.

As we touched on in Chapter 2, "What Are NFTs?" the demand for in-game items is massive. Gamers spent a collective $380 billion in 2020 on in-game digital assets. From avatar skins to weapons to extra lives, in-game items are a booming economy. There's no reason that many of these in-game items can't be NFTs, allowing users who've spent money in the game to resell their used or rarefied items.

Take the aforementioned Galaxy skin in Fortnite. The skin was released for only two weeks in August 2018. None have been created since then. By owning one, your clout (social credibility) instantly skyrockets among other players. While it's a rare item, the opportunities to capitalize on it are minimal. One day, a Fortnite marketplace might exist where owners of the Galaxy skin could resell this rare skin. And the NFT back-end would ensure that the skin was legitimate and not a fake. Who knows what it could fetch on the resale market? $10? $10,000? More?

What must be understood about shared metaverses is that people are there for a reason. They all have either a shared interest or a shared goal. As a result, there are hierarchies of participants within these communities. One factor that propels a player's rank in the game's hierarchy is their avatar's equipment. That's why people spend money on Fortnite skins that have no impact on actual gameplay. It's only natural that players in the future will truly own their items and have the ability to collect, buy, and sell them with other players.

A real-world example of this is SneakerCon. The sneaker collecting market is one of the more well-known and established collectible markets of the last decade. SneakerCon was created as a place where thousands of sneakerheads can convene in person to show off their sneakers. Some are looking to sell their sneakers. Some are looking to buy. Others even have stalls set up to sell shoe cleaning kits, sneaker artwork, and other businesses related to sneakers. But no matter who you are, if you're not showing up in your swaggiest pair of sneakers, then others won't take you seriously. SneakerCon is the physical equivalent of a metaverse for sneakerheads. People from all over go to SneakerCon to meet others with the same interest as them, make money, and build clout.

Another reason NFTs fit the metaverse is that many people are beginning to accumulate these digital assets. And that means these same people want to be able to show off their purchases. For instance, MetaKoven, the person who purchased Beeple's "Everydays: The First 5,000 Days" for more than $69 million, is turning the NFTs into a digital art gallery that can be viewed in metaverses like Decentraland.

As we've discussed, people collect for a variety of reasons. But there's one constant among all collectors: they want to display their collections.

Digital assets should be displayed in digital environments. Whether it's a virtual art gallery, an online video game, your very own virtual basement hangout, or some other virtual space that we cannot yet imagine, the metaverse is where we'll show off our NFTs.

And then there's the utility of NFTs in the metaverse.

Buying a Meebit NFT today gives you some clout, and it will go a long way 10 years from now when it's astonishing to own something that is hardly available. But Meebits are much more than simply cute collectibles. As mentioned in Chapter 6, "Creating and Minting NFTs," Meebits come with an OBJ file, so you have free reign to use your Meebit for whatever you'd like in any 3D environment.

We're not far away from some of these hit video games adding an open source element to the game where you can upload your own 3D-modeled items. We can envision NBA 2K gamers uploading their Meebits into the game and using them as their players.

This brings us to The Sandbox (and their comparables Decentraland, Somnium Space, and Axie Infinity), which is a living, breathing version of NFTs meets the metaverse. The Ethereum-based virtual world allows players to explore, interact, and play games, among other activities. Most notably, plots of LAND are bought and sold as NFTs on various marketplaces. Once you own LAND, you can develop it however you want—whether that's a house, a marketplace, or an application. You can lease the LAND, which is what WhaleShark (one of the largest LAND owners in The Sandbox) plans to do—leasing his LAND to artists and designers to build more value for other users in the game.

In many ways, The Sandbox is similar to Minecraft in its open nature of play. However, it differs in that it has its own in-game currency, $SAND, which can be traded on cryptocurrency exchanges, and you can actually own items in the game as NFTs. While it doesn't have the broad user appeal of a battle game like League of Legends or Fortnite, The Sandbox nailed down the in-game economy element of the metaverse, which is highly fascinating.

Look how much our behaviors have changed in the past decade, thanks to smartphones. The average person spends upward of 5–6 hours a day on their phone. Then if you group in the time we spend on our laptops, smart TVs, or streaming services, it becomes a lot easier to count the hours that we don't spend interacting with the Internet.

The Internet is our collective livelihood, and the evolution of the Internet is the metaverse. The same communities and areas where we spend our time on the Internet today will have a virtual component in the near future, if not already. And with these metaverses will come in-metaverse items that we want to own as NFTs.

It won't be absurd in the next 5–10 years to see an esports champion auction off NFTs of the weapons or items they used to win the title, in the same way that we auction off game-worn jerseys and game balls.

Non-bankable Assets

What are *nonbankable assets*? Assets such as rare collectibles (fine art, antiques, classic cars, jewelry, and the like), real estate, and intellectual property (copyrights, patents, and trademarks) are considered nonbankable. The reason these types of assets are nonbankable is that they're illiquid (there's no readily available market of buyers and sellers), usually require high investment capital, and often require intermediaries, either to buy or sell an asset and/or determine its value.

When we look 10–20 years into the future, the most widespread use of NFTs likely won't have anything to do with digital art. It will be the tokenization of physical items and intellectual property, made possible by an NFT's smart contract. This will lead to fractional ownership of things, thus increasing the pool of buyers and creating liquidity for a traditionally nonbankable asset.

Similar to what Uniswap did for small market cap cryptocurrency tokens, NFTs can do for nonbankable assets. Uniswap is one of the leading decentralized cryptocurrency exchanges, as opposed to a centralized exchange.

At *centralized exchanges*, such as Coinbase Pro or Binance, sellers post a price (usually in Bitcoin or Ethereum) at which they are willing to sell a particular cryptocurrency, together with an amount. This is the *ask price*. Similarly, buyers post a price at which they are willing to buy that cryptocurrency, together with an amount. This is the *bid price*. When the bid and ask match, the exchange of one cryptocurrency for the other takes place.

At *decentralized exchanges*, such as Uniswap, trades are drawn from pools of tokens. For example, if you wanted to buy AMP tokens, you would send Ethereum to the pool of Ethereum on Uniswap, and you would receive AMP from the pool of AMP tokens on Uniswap. The liquidity pools are provided by people who stake their tokens on Uniswap. *Staking* is like lending, and it allows Uniswap to use the staked tokens for trades. These pooled resources create the markets.

In return, those who staked their tokens receive a percentage of the trading fees that Uniswap charges. This provides an income stream opportunity for token holders, especially ones who planned to hold the token for months or years anyway.

Uniswap's protocols, which seamlessly handle all of these complexities, have created liquidity for tokens of all sizes, many of which are not on centralized exchanges, which generally focus only on high volume cryptocurrencies.

This same concept of creating liquidity for coins can be applied to the $78 trillion of nonbankable assets globally (as estimated by Accenture), the vast majority of which are highly illiquid. For example, unsurprisingly, there aren't many buyers out there for a $4.5 million 1955 Mercedes 300SL Gullwing or an expensive wine collection. They're illiquid assets.

But you can create liquidity for these higher-priced non-bankable assets by *tokenizing* them and thus fractionalizing the ownership. What does this mean? Let's take that $4.5 million 1955 Mercedes 300SL Gullwing. Are there a lot of people who would love to own this rare car? Probably millions. How many of those millions of people can afford it? Maybe a handful.

However, you can create one million NFTs, which would not only be collectibles, but each of which would represent 1/1,000,000 of that Mercedes valued at an initial price of $4.50. And now, anyone with five dollars can own part of that car. It's like a million of your closest friends pooling their money together to buy something nice. And all of a sudden, an illiquid asset becomes liquid.

This is what tokenizing a physical asset does. It opens up the market for more people to get involved in something that they cannot afford. Maybe on the opening day, all 1 million tokens are snatched up. Perhaps someone bought 500,000 of the tokens and hoarded them. As the number of people demanding that token (and wanting a slice of that Mercedes) goes up, so does the price of a token. Maybe a week later that Mercedes is now worth $5 million. A year later, it's $10 million. (Sounds a little like the stock market, right?)

What's interesting for assets like cars and real estate that get tokenized is that revenue streams can be tokenized as well. Let's say that 21st Century Fox is producing a heist movie and wants the stars to drive off into the sunset in the 1955 Mercedes 300SL Gullwing. The cost of renting that Mercedes is $100,000 for the day, which spread across the 1 million tokens grants $0.10 to every token you hold (or an immediate 2 percent return on your investment for the day). This model of additional revenue streams is especially appealing for fractionalized real estate.

The problem with nonbankable assets, as outlined by Accenture, is that:

> "Historically, it has been difficult to exploit the embedded value of non-bankable assets outside their traditional markets, limiting their role as collateral. The lack of consistent documentation, low trust, and pricing transparency as well as their high transactional costs and illiquidity have all tempered the interest of financial firms to include them as portfolio assets."

No matter what the nonbankable asset is, it can be "NFT-ed." And this opens up a huge opportunity for high net worth individuals to create liquidity for these assets that they have trouble using as collateral for a loan or selling off.

Why would people want to purchase nonbankable asset NFTs? According to Obrium research:

> "Value appreciation in passion investments has consistently outperformed the global equity markets over the past 15 years, growing 65% faster than the MSCI World index over that period."

Unfortunately, realizing this value is currently impossible until you sell the asset. By creating fractionalized ownership for the asset, you create liquidity. More people can buy and sell a part of that asset and drive the value upward if it's a desirable asset. And because there's now a liquid market for the NFTs that correlate to their asset, the owner no longer needs to find one buyer that would agree to the $4.5 million price tag of that Mercedes. The owner effectively found 1 million buyers who would collectively put up $5 million (or more) for the car.

When tokenizing a nonbankable asset, the owner isn't required to give up control of it. Suppose Mark Cuban wanted to fractionalize the ownership of the Dallas Mavericks. Theoretically, he could create 10,000 NFTs and now have a market to liquefy the value of all or a portion of the team.

Speed Bumps

There may be a speed bump on the road to fractionalizing nonbankable assets with NFTs. As we touched on in the previous chapter, fractionalizing assets with NFTs may cause the NFTs to be deemed securities by the SEC. They are akin to investments, after all. Such NFT drops may need to be registered with the SEC, which requires time, red tape, and legal costs. Or the NFT drop could potentially be done under one of the exceptions, such as Regulation D or Regulation A. Ideally, these processes would be streamlined in the future.

Additionally, securities can be traded only on securities exchanges that are registered with the SEC. So, current NFT marketplaces may need to register with the SEC to trade such NFTs, or new marketplaces that are registered with the SEC may need to come online.

NFTs representing real estate come with a different set of issues. Generally, deeds are recorded in a local county clerk's office. And deeds cannot be transferred unless state and local transfer taxes and fees are paid at the closing. A potential technical solution could be that real estate NFTs be held in multi-signature wallets, which are wallets where all parties must sign in order to approve transfers. The local governing authority could be an additional required signatory for any transfer of a real estate NFT.

Although the road to asset-backed NFTs may start out bumpy, we're optimistic that it will smooth out over time.

Digital Wallets

Your *digital wallet* is the new address and phone number for marketers, the new banking information for all payments, the new invoicing software for entrepreneurs, and much more. Knowing someone's digital wallet address is perhaps the single most valuable piece of information that you can have about a person in 2021 and beyond. Why? Digital wallets are the most effective way to connect directly with someone on many different levels. We just haven't realized it yet.

Gifts That Delight

If we wanted to connect with Mark Cuban to hear our business idea, we could tweet at him and hope he sees it. We could find him on Cyber Dust and try to get his attention. We could work our way up his chain of command through countless conversations with his associates. Or we could send him a thoughtful NFT directly to his digital wallet. And if the NFT delights him, he'll likely get in contact with us.

Knowing someone's digital wallet address gives you direct access to where they collect, where they bank, or where they do business. It's the new phone number, address, banking information, and so forth for savvy marketers.

We're not far away from seeing the first marketing campaign delivered entirely as NFTs.

For example, say Taco Bell is debuting a new food item. Instead of blasting the message out on Facebook ads or during TV commercial breaks, they could take a different approach. They could design a piece of digital artwork featuring the new food item, mint it as an NFT, add some perks around owning the NFT, and then send the promotional NFT directly to thousands of people's digital wallets.

Granted, the cost of gas fees for sending out thousands of "digital ads" would be far more expensive than the cost of delivering a Facebook ad to the same number of people. But if executed correctly, the press and buzz it creates in the crypto and NFT communities, along with the guarantee of mainstream media covering this absurdity, would far outweigh the cost.

The previous example is theoretical, of course. But it's not that crazy when you think of a digital wallet as a very personal asset holder for individuals. It's a direct connection to a person's finances and their collection of holdings.

And so, whether you're looking to connect with someone you could never get a hold of through traditional means or you are looking for a new and refreshing way to delight someone with gifts, the digital wallet is the way to go.

The downside to this could be when gas fees are significantly reduced or become virtually nonexistent. As we discussed in Chapter 3, "Why NFTs Have Value," Ethereum will be switching over to proof of stake, which will significantly reduce gas fees. And transaction fees on WAX and other proof-of-stake blockchains are already minimal. So, why are low gas fees a downside? One word: spam. Just like those unsolicited, annoying marketing emails that clog up your inbox, we, unfortunately, see the same for NFTs.

Many cryptocurrencies have been airdropping their tokens to digital wallets for years now. NFTs won't be any different. But it will likely be a minor nuisance like spam email is today. Similar to email spam blockers, NFT spam blockers will be developed as well.

The Future of Payments

Undoubtedly, Cash App, Venmo, PayPal, Zelle, and countless other peer-to-peer payment apps are practical and accessible. Creating invoices and billing people through QuickBooks or FreshBooks is familiar and trusted. But these are centralized. As you may recall in Chapter 3, we discussed the advantages of making payments via a decentralized system such as a blockchain.

Now, remembering someone's 42-character digital wallet address is trickier than finding their Venmo username. However, with blockchain domain names, you can simplify the way of reaching someone's digital wallet. For example, when you want to send crypto to a digital wallet, in the field where you would put their wallet address, you can type in **QuHarrison.eth**, and it will autopopulate Qu's address. A URL is now the new way of sending money back and forth.

When you couple peer-to-peer digital wallet payments with NFTs, we effectively have an entirely new way for businesses to offer services and charge customers.

As you may recall from Chapter 6, Gary Vaynerchuk's VeeFriends NFTs provide a new means of selling his consulting and other services. There's no reason that agencies, ranging from PR services to growth consulting, cannot adopt this same model. Agencies of the future will forgo all need for a bank and expensive billing software, using NFT smart contracts and digital wallets to transact directly with their customers.

This vision, of course, makes sense only if everyone has a digital wallet, which is a lot closer than you think, given that Big Tech already has their hands in the pie.

Apple, Google, and Samsung all have mobile wallets loaded natively on their smartphones—not in the sense of a cryptocurrency digital wallet, but rather the digitization of credit cards, boarding passes, gift cards, and anything you might find in your wallet (aside from your ID). The idea is that the smartphone has already replaced hundreds of other technologies, so why not our wallets too?

While paying for things with your phone was a hard pill to swallow for many at first, COVID-19 drastically accelerated the adoption of mobile payments. Go to an airport and count the number of people who have their boarding pass in their Apple Wallet. It's more than the number of people who print out a ticket. Mobile wallets are a bridge to the world of crypto and NFT wallets. Quite literally, Apple Wallet is a couple of integrations away from being the largest NFT wallet out there.

The Unwritten Future of NFTs

The beauty of NFTs is that their future isn't chiseled in stone. Nobody knows what will become the most prominent use of NFTs. Essentially, risk-takers are writing the future of NFTs— the ones who are trying new things, coming up with radical applications for NFTs, taking NFTs to places we haven't thought of, or simply executing a sound strategy better than everyone else.

The NFT-ification of everything will take place over the next decade. And anyone can participate. The future of NFTs is being written as we speak.

Let's write it together.

Index